V. Interesting! £4.00

Mull of Kintyre to Moosburg

Memories of Peace and War: 1914-1945

Mull of Kintyre

to

Moosburg

Memories of Peace and War: 1914-1945

Lachlan B Young

Perth and Kinross District Libraries
1994

ISBN 0 905452 15 1

Published by
Perth and Kinross District Libraries
Perth

Printed by
Cordfall Ltd
041 332 4640

To
Alison,
Rory and
Andrew
in memory of happy holidays

Contents

Illustrations

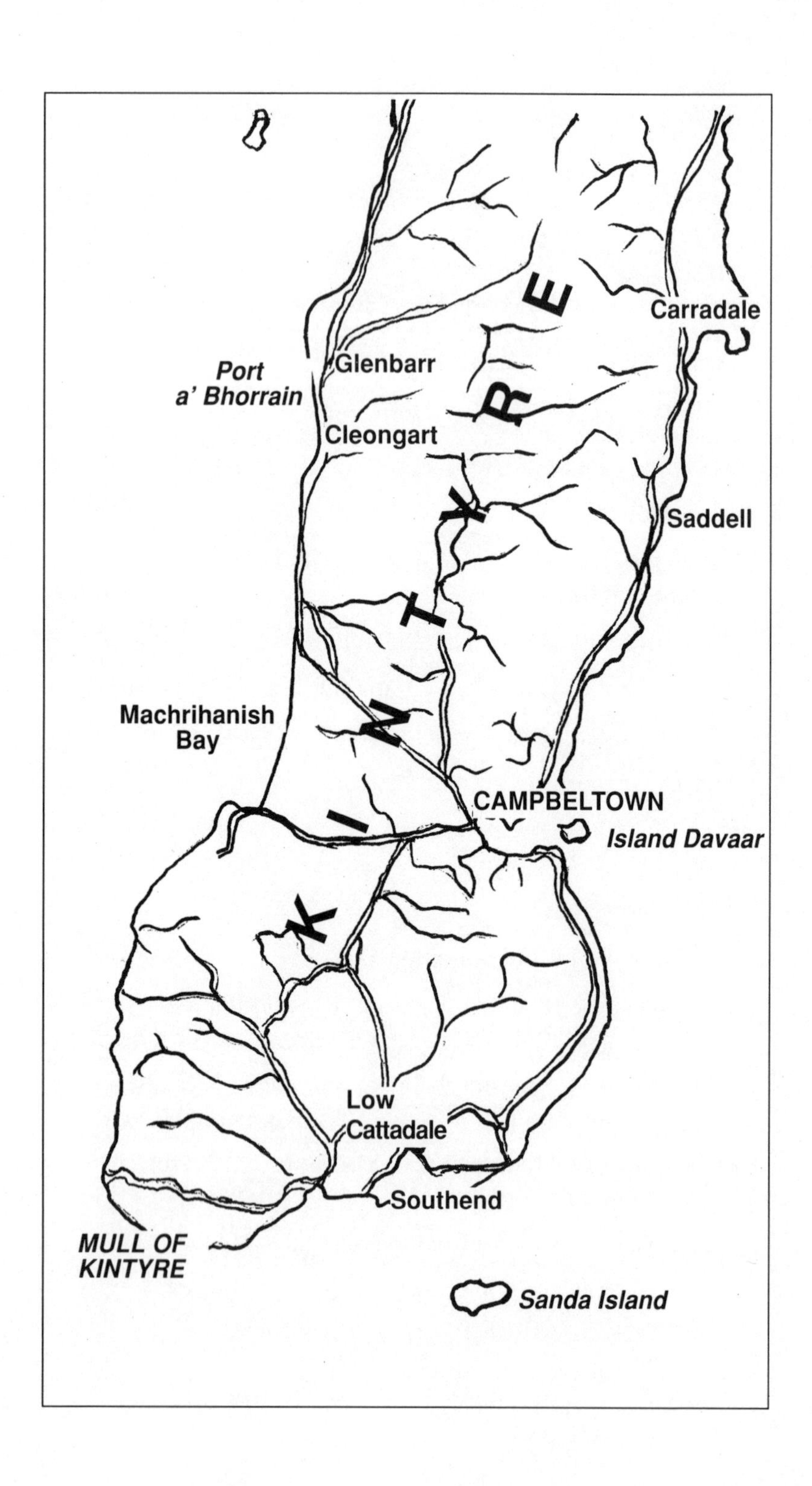
KINTYRE
Carradale
Port
a' Bhorrain
Glenbarr
Cleongart
Saddell
Machrihanish
Bay
CAMPBELTOWN
Island Davaar
Low
Cattadale
Southend
MULL OF
KINTYRE
Sanda Island

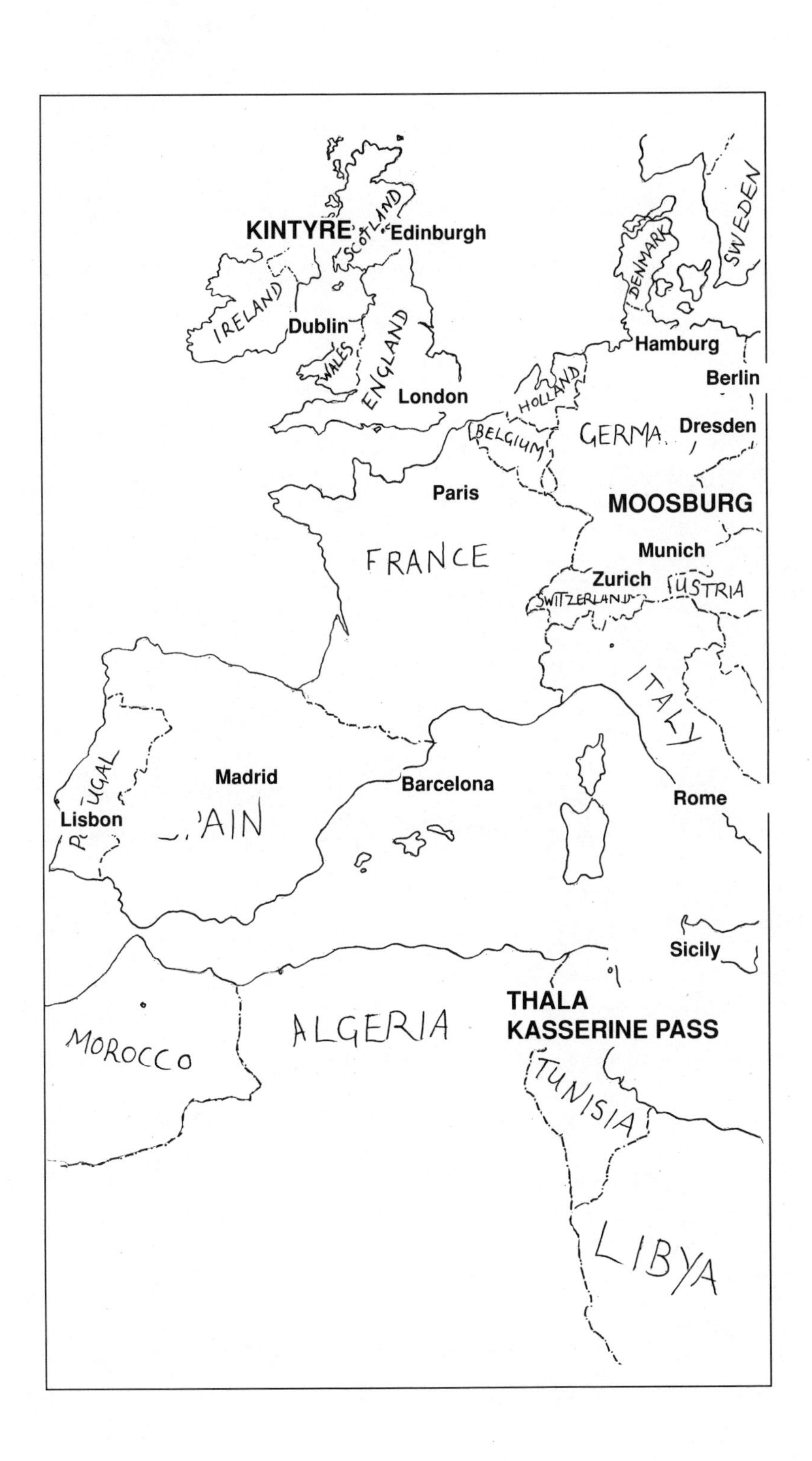

KINTYRE
SCOTLAND
Edinburgh
IRELAND
Dublin
WALES
ENGLAND
London
DENMARK
SWEDEN
Hamburg
Berlin
HOLLAND
BELGIUM
Dresden
Paris
MOOSBURG
Munich
FRANCE
Zurich
SWITZERLAND
ITALY
Madrid
Barcelona
Lisbon
Rome
Sicily
THALA
KASSERINE PASS
ALGERIA
MOROCCO
TUNISIA
LIBYA

Acknowledgements

I wish to acknowledge with grateful thanks the invaluable assistance received from the Perth and Kinross District Librarian and his staff in the preparation of this book.

For some of the illustrations used in the book, thanks are due to the following organisations:–

The Imperial War Museum for pictures of British and German tanks, and a map of Tunisia showing the disposition of opposing forces at the battles of Kasserine and Thala.

Perth Museum and Art Gallery for pictures of a blacksmith at work and a travelling mill in operation.

The Scottish Museum Archive for pictures of a binder and reaper.

Preface

THIS IS LACHIE'S BOOK. In spite of his distinguished designations and degrees, he has always been Lachie to me. He and my brother Archie were about three years younger than I was, but we shared not only a less than wealthy upbringing in Southend, near the Mull of Kintyre – in a material sense – but also academic and sporting pursuits in the outer world. 'Pacifists' as we fondly called ourselves while students in the early nineteen-thirties, we still went to war together to defeat Nazi-ism. Archie did not come back.

Lachie's book contains a wonderful evocation of Scottish farming life at the beginning of the century; one which should prove invaluable to social historians in years to come. I can vouch for its accuracy in every astonishing detail; but then nothing less would I expect from a boy who became a man always imbued with honesty and integrity, a legacy perhaps from his Covenanting forebears.

But is Lachie's book all staid and stolid stuff? By no means. His stories of our youthful forays to the Highland Games, when he and Archie and I ran and jumped, and Hamish (who later became a Lt. Col. and Convener of Argyll County Council) threw weights about are full of excitement. One tells of the tabloid-scandal which visited him and Archie when, after winning prizes of ten shillings (50p) at the local sports, they were branded 'professionals' by an anonymous 'clype' and had to seek re-instatement as amateurs.

But has the book not – like most other contemporary tales – some reference to sex and violence? Of course it has. Violence?

Read about Lachie's boyhood adventure when sent on a rickety old bicycle to collect two ferrets from a hill farm. Read also about his experiences as a young soldier at war with the acrid stench of death around him. I can vouch for the complete accuracy of this as well. He and I received no counselling or psychiatric comforting when we returned to 'civvie street'. We did have the Church, however. And sex? Read about what happened to Lachie as a senior schoolboy when he kissed his first girl.

Lachie's book is a splendid book, full of humanity and intimations of Scotland's heritage.

Dr. Angus MacVicar

Introduction
It Seems Like Yesterday

IN COURSE OF MY working life, thirty years of which were spent in educational administration, there always seemed to be more work than time; so work was carried home at nights and holidays were cut short. These bad habits found no favour with my wife who rightly complained, especially when the children were young, that the claims of office work all too often took precedence over the claims of family life. As I approached retirement and the prospect of more time for leisure pursuits, my wife and I decided to invest in a two-berth caravan which we were convinced would be the most economical way to travel round the countryside, enable us to enjoy longer holidays and give us independence, self-catering and freedom to move when and where we felt inclined. Rather to my surprise we both became caravan addicts and, as it proved simple to hitch and unhitch and easy to trail behind a car, we kept it and put it to use for more than fifteen years. For some years our status as grandparents gave us an opportunity to enhance our pleasure by sharing the company of three grandchildren on holiday. From their infancy we enjoyed looking after them from time to time, but it was a special joy when, during their primary school stage, they made plain their wish to share in our caravan holidays. We bought an awning, camp beds and sleeping bags in which the children could gain an impression that they were camping out, while still attached to the caravan. For them and us it proved to be great fun. Our favourite caravan site with the grandchildren adjoined a stretch of rugged countryside over which I frequently took the children on what we called 'adventure walks', while telling them stories many of which related to my own childhood.

It was during these walks and talks with the grandchildren that it first occurred to me how wide was the gap between their childhood and mine, and how very different the conditions in which we were born and brought up. They had been born and brought up in towns and enjoyed the amenities and social opportunities of life in towns; but to me who had been born and brought up on a small farm in South Argyllshire, about three miles from the nearest village and ten miles from the nearest town, it was obvious that my grandchildren lacked the rich background of country life which I had enjoyed, while it was equally obvious that they enjoyed many opportunities and advantages of which I, in my rural childhood, had been utterly deprived. Quite apart from the differences between town and country life, there lay between their childhood and mine a vast gulf of which they were wholly unaware and which they could not be expected to bridge. The gulf was one partly of culture and mode of life, but mainly of wealth and material progress or, perhaps more accurately, of economic and technical change.

When I was a young child there were in my rural district no motor cars, trucks or coaches, no aeroplanes, no tractors, no gas or electricity, no roads paved with tarmacadam or asphalt, no cinema or theatre, no radio or television and very few telephones. In our local school we still had dry closets and few houses in the district as yet had bathrooms. I was part of the last generation whose early childhood was spent in the age of the horse and cart.

It is not easy for children who live in the age of the computer, television and video-recorder to grasp fully what it was like to spend one's childhood quite unaware of the amenities and material goods which they take for granted. But luckily for the children of my generation, just because we were unaware, we did not feel deprived of the many material advances which still lay in the future. It is equally difficult for children now growing up to grasp fully the huge changes which have taken place in the value of money since the beginning of the twentieth century. When I was young a penny £ $^{1}/_{240}$ was pocket-money with which a child could buy a choice of things at the village shop. An experienced farm ploughman might receive in wages about one pound per week plus a rent-free cottage, milk and potatoes; while a maidservant who lived in might receive ten shillings (50p) per week. A University graduate at the peak of his or her career would be very content to earn £1,000 per annum, but not many attained such heights. Perhaps never in the course of one lifetime has there been in Britain such a drastic change in the value of money. For many elderly people it has been more difficult to adjust to that change than to all the material and technological changes which have occurred during the same period. It was the realisation of these many changes in course of my lifetime which gave me the urge to record, for the interest of my grandchildren (and perhaps of their children) some of the memories of my youth.

Chapter 1
O' Hame and Infancy

MY EARLIEST MEMORY is of sitting under the large table in the farm kitchen, playing with a fox terrier called 'Dougie' and a wooden eggcup of the kind that could take an egg at either end. I was probably between two and three years old. As I sat there I could watch my father's legs stumping between the kitchen range and the kitchen sink or the dresser, while he made the breakfast for the whole family, including the farm workers who took their meals with the family. Breakfast always included a large pot of oatmeal porridge, followed by a cooked dish such as home-cured bacon, eggs, kippers, liver and kidneys or farm cheese toasted in front of the kitchen fire till it bubbled on the large enamelled plate. It was a large, nourishing and tasty meal which laid the foundation for hard physical labour throughout the day. The men, who included the grown-ups of the family and the male farm servants, had breakfast first, starting about 7am; the women and children followed after, but for everyone breakfast was a hearty meal.

My father, who lived for ninety years, made a habit all his life of eating a large helping of porridge twice each day, for breakfast and supper; and one of the few treats which he gave himself was occasionally to pour a ladle of cream from the cheese vat into a bowl and then eat his porridge by dipping each spoonful into the cream. That, I can assure you is porridge for a gourmet, although perhaps advisable only for those who are constantly engaged in physical labour.

My father's farm was mainly a dairy farm, and he became responsible for making the breakfast because he was unable to help with the milking of the cows. He could not milk cows because he could not bend his right leg the knee-joint of which was locked. This disability he had suffered shortly before I was born. At that time my father had not secured the tenancy of a farm but he was managing two farms which belonged, as did most of the farms in the district, to the Duke of Argyll. These two farms were about three miles apart and he and his family lived in one of the farm houses. As each farm had livestock, he had to travel daily between the two farms to ensure the welfare of the livestock and this he usually did on foot.

On the occasion which led to his disability he began early in the morning by driving some animals on foot over ten miles to market in Campbeltown. He then walked home, had a meal, walked three miles to the second farm, looked over the livestock, including the sheep on the hill ground, and then walked home. He had walked over thirty miles in course of the day. Towards the end of this long day of walking a blister was raised on his right heel, and dye from the new socks which his wife had knitted for him seeped into the wound causing septicaemia, or blood poisoning as it was then called. Because he was too busy to seek treatment, he was seriously ill before the gravity of the situation was realised and hospital treatment was begun. Although he came within an ace of losing his leg, and indeed his life, his inherent fitness carried him through and he survived with two large depressions in his leg where drainage tubes had been inserted and with a knee-joint which was locked for life.

Perhaps due to his own upbringing in a family whose religious beliefs and mode of living were akin to those of the Free Presbyterian Church of today, my father was very strict about the standards of behaviour which he expected from his children. My grandfather, John Young and my grandmother, Jean Gemmell were, as were many other families in Kintyre, the descendants of forebears who had migrated, mainly in the seventeenth and eighteenth centuries, from farming stock in Ayrshire and Renfrewshire to take up tenancies of farms in Kintyre. At least some of them had been encouraged to do so by a Duke of Argyll who was sympathetic to their religious beliefs, while they in turn had been instrumental in attracting others to Kintyre. As far as I can gather my grandfather's family had covenanting sympathies, and he was so strongly attached to the United Presbyterian Church that he insisted on driving his family by wagonette and pony to worship in the nearest United Presbyterian Church, which was twelve miles distant in Campbeltown. There in the Lowland Kirk the family attended morning and afternoon services every Sunday before driving the twelve miles home to their farm.

While the Sabbath was strictly observed, the other six days of the week were spent in hard physical labour; for in those days large stones were still being dug from the fields and carried by horse sled to the boundaries, where they were built into dry-stone dykes. The land was fertilised partly by farmyard manure and partly by loads of seaweed carted from the beach during the winter, and any time left from the constant routine of farm work was spent in digging field drains and boundary ditches to remove surplus water from the land. Because my grandfather insisted on working outside even in the wettest and stormiest weather, and thoroughly soaked for hours on end, he finally contracted an illness which affected his kidneys and bladder and he died before reaching old age. If he had been less obsessed with the need for constant labour and had spared a little more time for leisure, my grandfather might have lived, as did my other three grandparents, beyond ninety years of age.

I recall my father telling me of an occasion, when he was in his late teens, and some of his friends had gathered on a Saturday night, after a week of hard work, around the kitchen table in Cleongart, my grandfather's farm. One of the lads had brought a pack of playing cards, which my father claimed was the first deck of cards he had ever seen, and four of the young men began to play a game of whist while the others looked on. As my grandfather had been busy with some work among the cattle he did not enter the kitchen until after 9pm. He looked at the game for a few minutes, then without warning he gathered up the cards from the table, threw them into the kitchen fire, uttered the stern rebuke: 'Ye'll no play that Deil's game in my hoose on a Seturday night!' and walked out of the kitchen to his bedroom to prepare for the Sabbath. 'That', remarked my father, 'was the last time the Saturday night party gathered round the kitchen table at Cleongart.'

After my grandfather's death the real authority in the management of the farm was assumed by my grandmother, a small woman with a strong, stubborn nature and afraid of neither man nor beast. She had brought up a family of four sons and four daughters but, when her sons married they left home to find other employment, until she was left with two unmarried daughters and hired men to run the farm. When I was at school my brothers and I were invited to stay, during the summer holidays, for a week at each of the farms run by our two grandmothers, and that was our only holiday away from home. An incident at Grandma Young's farm, Cleongart, has remained firmly in my memory. The milk cows at the farm were served by an Ayrshire bull who was growing old and, especially in hot weather, unpredictable in temper. Since my aunts feared the bull, one of the hired men was assigned the task of driving the cows from the pasture to the byre for the evening milking. On this occasion when the ploughman entered the field the bull charged, and the man was lucky to escape over the gate. When he reported to Grandma Young that the bull had chased him, she grabbed a strong hazel stick, marched about two hundred yards down to the field, flung open the gate, walked straight at the bull, yelling and flourishing the stick. The bull and the cows started running and not one of them stopped until they were in the byre and all standing quietly in their usual stall. To me that incident typifies my grandmother.

My other grandmother with whom we spent a week of the summer holidays was Grandma Black, whose maiden name was Margaret Johnston, married to Grandpa Donald Black, who was tenant of a small farm named Dalkeith, but usually known as Port a'Bhorrain, which was really a tiny inlet of the sea close to the farm house. Port a'Bhorrain was a rather isolated farm, bounded on the west by a rocky shore facing the Atlantic, on the east by a raised beach and on the south by a small river with deep, rocky pools in which salmon, trout and eels could be seen moving around in the peat-coloured water. To my brothers and me the rocky shore, with its variety of shells and sea creatures, and the deep pools in the river were sources of endless interest, because we loved to collect shells and pebbles and we were very keen on catching fish, either with our hands or with a loop of copper wire. Every farm in those days had a ready supply of copper wire in the form of rabbit snares, which could be unravelled to provide single strands of wire.

Although I was unaware of it at the time I learned later that Grandma Black was much younger than Grandpa Black who, by the time we went to the farm on holiday, was suffering from an advanced stage of what was then called Palsy but was probably Parkinson's syndrome. Although his head and hands were subject to continuous tremor and he was virtually confined to an armchair, he yet had a long life and died in his ninety seventh year. Grandma Black was quite different from Grandma Young, who was a small bundle of energy and temper, while Grandma Black was taller and had a natural reserve and dignity, although extremely kind and motherly. The old social values she accepted without question; for her the pillars of the community were the laird, the minister, the doctor and the schoolmaster in that order. I recall the first time, when on holiday, we brought her a salmon which we had pulled from the river, instead of praise which we had expected we received a rare scolding, including the rebuke: 'What would the laird say if he knew; he might have us out of the farm!' It would have shocked her to learn that we were not worried about what the laird thought, so long as neither he nor his gamekeeper caught us catching his salmon.

Although by the time I knew her she was not a regular attender at church, Grandma Black's Christian faith was simple and sure; her belief rested on a knowledge of the Bible which she had read from childhood and her acceptance of its teaching was unclouded by any shadow of doubt. Whenever I have looked back over my own life I have always envied that sure belief in ultimate goodness which enabled Grandma to sustain with quiet dignity the family sorrows and trials of which she had to bear her full share. Although she came from a family which had a reputation for being clever, she never allowed her undoubted intelligence to undermine the sureness of her faith and the simple goodness of her way of life. The family of eight children who were brought up at Port a'Bhorrain comprised two sons and six daughters. One son and one daughter remained unmarried; the other six married and had families. The second daughter, Euphemia Barbara Black, whom the family called Babbie, grew up to marry Robert Young, the oldest son of the family at Cleongart, and thus became my mother.

Cleongart was less than two miles from Port a'Bhorrain and between them was another farm, Barrmains, which was occupied by a family named Black who were cousins of the family at Port a'Bhorrain. When the mother of the family at Barrmains sadly died while some of her family were still young, my mother, who was then a girl in her late teens, volunteered to move in with the family as their housekeeper. Although excellent training for her later role as wife and mother, the task of looking after a large family of men and boys was a heavy responsibility for one so young. As two of the sons at Barrmains were close friends of my father, he was a frequent visitor at Barrmains where he met and fell in love with the young housekeeper who was to become his wife and my mother.

Many years later I heard my father say that the two sons at Barrmains who were his closest friends made plans to emigrate to Zimbabwe (then the colony entitled Southern Rhodesia), which was being opened up after the Boer War for settlement by farmers, and that he would certainly have gone with them had he not been engaged to marry my mother. One of these two brothers, Duncan Black, later became among the largest landowners in Rhodesia, with a holding of separate farms extending over thousands of hectares of good arable land. Mainly through their influence many young men from Kintyre later emigrated to Rhodesia to become farmers and most of them prospered. Among them was my mother's brother, Donald Black, who became one of the prosperous farmers in Rhodesia.

Robert Young and Barbara Black were married in 1903. In the hope of gaining the tenancy of a farm my father made contact with the Factor of the Duke of Argyll, who owned the majority of farms in Kintyre. Although he was not given the immediate tenancy of a farm, he was appointed manager of two farms in the parish of Southend, which were about three miles apart. When he had proved his ability as a manager of land and livestock, he was given the tenancy of Low Cattadale which he occupied for the rest of his working life, and there, except for my brother John, my brothers and sisters and I were born and brought up.

I was born in March, 1911, the fifth of seven children, and when I had reached my fifth birthday, in the middle of the 1914-18 war, my family consisted of father, mother, five sons, two daughters, two menservants and one maidservant. I include the hired staff because they were treated as part of the family; they slept in the farm house, they usually took their meals with the family and they took a genuine interest in the work of the farm and in the livestock, especially the horses. The seven children were John, Donald, Margaret (Meg), Robert, Lachie, Tom and Jean who was only a few months old. When the younger manservant was called up for military service, men were so scarce that my father sought to get my eldest brother, John, exempted from attendance at school to secure his full-time help in the work of the farm. Although I had just begun attendance at school, I can still recall my father discussing with my mother his meeting with the headmaster who had protested vigorously about the removal from school of the boy whom he regarded as his brightest pupil. But his protest was in vain for John was allowed to leave school before he attained the age of fourteen.

Although my father required his children to work on the farm and around the farm steading up to the limit of their strength, and all of us from five years onwards had our daily rota of duties to perform, he was a very kindly man with a ready sense of fun and warm sympathy with any disability or weakness; but I am sure his devotion to work was conditioned by his own upbringing by a father for whom hard work took second place only to religious observance. Yet my father had apparently been given the opportunity to adopt a career other than farming. In his local rural school he showed such promise that his headmaster recommended his transfer to an academic course in a secondary school. To this his father would not agree because he would have had to live away from home; but five miles away there was a rural headmaster who was a classical scholar and who promised that, if the boy attended his school, he would give him tuition that would enable him to pass University preliminary examinations. My father travelled daily to this school on the stage coach which ran between Campbeltown and Tarbert at times which enabled the headmaster to give him individual tuition after school hours. His academic progress was satisfactory until he chanced to hear his father tell a prominent member of his church that he had a great ambition to see his son, Robert, train to be a minister of the United Presbyterian Church. From that time he became so rebellious at school that he was asked to leave and so ended his formal education.

After leaving school he was required to labour as hard as his father and gained experience of every aspect of farm work from ploughing to harvesting; draining, dyking and fencing; working with cattle and pigs; shepherding from lambing to clipping and dipping; and the use and maintenance of farm implements. As we, his children, grew up and started learning the many skills needed to perform all the tasks on a farm, we often found it hard to match, and sometimes none of us could reach, the standards which our father set himself in everyday work. A scythe, for example, is now almost a museum piece, but when I was young it was an implement used from hay-time to harvest-time, and I assume there must have been the occasional person (though I failed to meet him) who could wield a scythe with the perfect rhythm shown by my father, and who could whet it to an edge like a razor, which enabled him to cut grass as short and smooth as a lawn mower, and to cut all day without showing signs of weariness. Although in that skill I could not even approach his mastery, nor could any of my brothers, I took some pride in finally matching his skill (which required something of the same rhythm) at sowing grain evenly across a five-yard rig with two hands, while carrying a loaded, kidney-shaped hopper slung from both shoulders. That skill became outmoded when my father acquired a machine for sowing grain. In the same way the reaper, followed later by the binder, reduced the need to acquire skill in the use of a scythe. The combine harvester did not appear until after I had grown up and left the farm.

In the little leisure time which he could snatch from labouring on the family farm my father managed to acquire skill in two related activities: one was in Scottish country dancing which he kept up in adult life until one of his knee-joints became locked as a result of septicaemia; the other was playing Scottish music on the fiddle, which remained his chief recreation until his fingers became stiff with age and manual labour on the farm. When young he saved over a long period the little money he was given until he was able to buy an old fiddle, and then with little help he taught himself to play entirely by ear. His talent must have been quite marked, for he could play fluently and with feeling a wide range of Scottish dance music, pipe music and slow airs with which he had become familiar solely by listening. Even in later life he did not own a record player nor had he ever learnt to read music. When I was old enough to reflect on such things I watched with admiration on an evening as my father took his fiddle down from the shelf in the farm kitchen, strummed the strings with his thumb and proceeded to tune it to his satisfaction without the aid of a tuning fork or a piano. That kind of musical talent was beyond my reach and my understanding, yet I listened with great pleasure while he played, and also when he sang in his untutored tenor voice. To my knowledge he was never a member of a choir, yet in church or concert hall he would listen for a few minutes then sing a tenor part without the slightest difficulty. That his musical talent was not passed on to me is one of my abiding regrets, yet I was delighted, as I know my father would have been, when musical ability emerged in his grandson and, since it comes from both sides of the family, has emerged even more strongly in his great-grandchildren.

While I admired my father and was much attached to him, some of my child hood memories of him are far from pleasant; for despite his strong sense of fun and his sympathy with real suffering and misfortune, he had a quick temper and a heavy hand which he used without the slightest hesitation to slap head or bottom when he found us breaking the rules or up to serious mischief. When out-of-doors he almost always carried a stick or shepherd's crook, which he would wield over his sons' buttocks when he thought such punishment was merited. And I must confess it usually was.

My memories of my mother are all too few and, with one exception, they are redolent of love and joy and comfort and laughter. To her husband and seven children she gave all the attention and care and time that they needed, and that despite the many hours she had to spend, every day in the week, in supervising the household, milking cows twice daily, making cheese and butter and sterilizing all the dairy utensils. She remains in my memory as a lovely lady, with a mass of light-brown hair which gleamed in the light, brown eyes which often smiled and a ready ripple of laughter. She was trim of figure and quick of movement but had the calm temperament of Grandma Black and was not easily roused to anger. The only occasion on which I can recall my mother giving me a smacking has remained firmly in my memory, because the punishment was as unexpected as it was well-deserved. In the farm kitchen there was a handsome, two-tiered dresser, the lower tier comprising two cupboards surmounted by three drawers. While the dresser was of pine, the three drawers were stained in a warm reddish-brown colour. It happened that the ebony finger board of my father's fiddle had become loose and had been left on the dresser until he could find time to replace it. At that time I was about four years old and was playing alone in the kitchen while my older brothers and sister were at school. My mother was busy in the dairy making cheese while my younger brother was playing round her feet. I managed to climb on to a chair to get hold of the ebony finger board, with the sharp corner of which I proceeded to decorate the front of the three drawers by hitting them as hard as I could, leaving them deeply pock-marked. I then went down to the dairy and invited my mother to come and admire my handiwork. When she found time she came to the kitchen, took one look at the dresser and then, to my amazement and distress, gave me a good smacking on the bottom. Since at that time I wore a grey, tweed kilt, with no underwear, the 'skelping' took full effect on my bare bottom.

Chapter 2
The Wee School

IT MUST HAVE BEEN some relief to my mother when I reached school age and she no longer had to guard against my mischief-making while the school was in session. Although I was a rather thin and weakly child compared with my brothers, I joined them in their daily trek to school at the beginning of May following my fifth birthday. As the local school was about two miles from our farm we had a daily walk of about four miles, which was quite far enough for a five-year old child. Yet some of the children at our school had to walk up to eight miles daily from the age of five. The family whom we most envied lived on a sheep farm about six miles from the school, so they had the privilege of travelling to and from school in a buggy drawn by a little pony, driven by the eldest brother and stabled in a farm stable close to the school. In those days there was no public transport in the district.

When I was a child the primary school was known as the elementary school, which most of the children in rural areas attended up to the school leaving age of fourteen. Only a small minority of children transferred to a secondary school at about the age of twelve, provided they had passed a qualifying examination, and many who passed this examination did not choose, or were not allowed by their parents, to transfer to secondary school for one of two reasons: either because their parents insisted on their leaving school and starting work at the earliest possible date, or because attendance at the nearest secondary school in Campbeltown required pupils to live in lodgings during the week, which was beyond the means of poorer parents. Because a number of very clever pupils left school at the age of fourteen to become apprentices or farm workers, the rural districts enjoyed the benefit of having some very able craftsmen and some very able shepherds and farm workers. To regard rural workers in general as inferior beings or clodhoppers was a gross misjudgement, since many had the ability though they lacked the opportunity to gain professional qualifications. Those pupils who remained in the elementary school after the age of twelve were placed in what were called supplementary classes, where the ablest reached a good standard in basic subjects such as English and Mathematics. If a parent died or a family became destitute, a child might be granted exemption from attendance at school before attaining the age of fourteen.

When I was a child there was no immunisation or vaccination except against smallpox; immunity from a disease was usually acquired by surviving an attack of that disease, and not all survived. It was taken for granted that children at school would become infected from time to time by diseases of varying severity including diphtheria, measles, mumps, rubella, scarlet fever and whooping cough. Scarcely a year passed without at least one of these maladies reaching epidemic proportions and almost any one of them, especially diphtheria and scarlet fever, could prove fatal. On occasions a child would become infected with two of these diseases at the same time and the symptoms of one could disguise the other, while increasing the severity of the illness. I recall that the children of our family contracted mumps and scarlet fever at the same time and scarlet fever was not diagnosed until, as we slowly recovered, patches of skin began to peel from the palms of our hands and the soles of our feet.

In the Autumn after I enrolled at school my family were infected with whooping cough. All of them except me made a good recovery, but in my case the cough was so severe and dragged on for so long that I was kept at home all winter and was unable to attend school until the following Spring. I had barely recovered from whooping cough when all the children were struck down with measles. My younger sister was a babe in arms when my mother was burdened with the additional task of having to nurse the whole family through measles. Just as her children were recovering from this attack, which was quite serious, our mother, exhausted by her burdens as housewife, mother and nurse, in addition to years of constant labour in byre and dairy, was herself stricken by illness. Almost certainly as a result of overwork and exhaustion her illness developed into pneumonia affecting both lungs, for which at that time there was no specific therapy. Despite her robust constitution her condition deteriorated and, in the week in which I reached my sixth birthday, she died.

No loss and no sorrow that I have suffered in the rest of my life can compare with the death of my mother. Only someone who, as a child, has had to endure the death of a dearly-loved mother can fully share the feelings of emptiness and desolation which seemed to get deeper as the months passed. Years later I was able to appreciate that my older brothers and sister, because of their greater understanding, may have suffered at the time even more than I did; but for weeks I was shut in with my own grief, enduring all the pain and emptiness which came from knowing that mother had gone away and would never again be there to love and comfort me. Because I had been in poor health throughout the previous winter, and was still weakly at the time of mother's death, perhaps I was more than normally sensitive to the loss of all the care and love which had been lavished on me. As the months and years passed I began to accept that the sense of loss would always be there and that something of the glad, joyous morning of life had gone for ever. Even now, in my old age, if I let my memory linger too long on the death of my mother I can feel tears welling up behind my eyelids.

Although I was not allowed to attend my mother's funeral service, I can still recall the day because, on that evening, for the only time in my life I saw my father in tears. Of course I was not old enough to have any conception of the tragic loss which he had suffered, the utter devastation which he must have felt and the gravity of the burden which he had to bear as the sole parent of a family of seven children, the eldest a boy of fourteen and the youngest a baby girl scarcely one year old, and as a hard-working farmer who had lost his equally hard-working wife and partner and had to strive, without much working capital, to secure enough staff to run the farm with the economy and efficiency required to make a living for himself and his family. In the years of depression which afflicted farming soon after the end of the 1914-18 war, that was by no means an easy task. Shortly after the death of his wife my father was summoned for interview by a war-service tribunal, who had the task of selecting those to be called up for military service. If my father had been enlisted for military service his family would have been left destitute. Fortunately for us the tribunal decided, after learning of his bereavement, his family circumstances and the physical disability of his locked knee joint, that he should go home to look after his children and his farm. The fact that my father was even considered for war service was clear evidence of the urgent demand for recruits to the army in 1918.

At the beginning of May, after my mother's death, I resumed attendance at school. During my long absence I had become fairly fluent in reading and, by listening to my older brothers and sister learning their homework, I could recite the multiplication tables as well as a number of hymns and psalms and answers to some of the questions in the shorter catechism. I knew by rote 'what was the chief end of man' (although much puzzled as to the meaning of that short word 'end') and I could recite the definitions of 'Justification', 'Adoption' and 'Sanctification', although without the slightest notion of the meaning of these very condensed definitions composed by scholarly theologians, which were probably beyond the under-standing of many adults, and certainly beyond the comprehension of the pupils in elementary schools who were compelled to memorise them and physically punished when they failed. I have always been fascinated by the sound of words and found it fairly easy to remember phrases and quotations and to learn passages by rote. It was a gift which proved useful in later life, especially as a student when one had to acquire the art of impressing the examiner.

Despite my age and my assorted scraps of knowledge, on my return to school I was placed with the small group of beginners, which proved very tiresome for me as well as for the teacher of the younger children who was the headmaster's wife. Trouble arose from my boredom and my inability to keep my mouth shut. When a fellow-pupil failed to recognise a three-letter or longer word I would immediately blurt out the answer, which so annoyed our teacher that she would take me by the ear, and pull me round behind the blackboard where I could not see the words which were printed on large sheets like wall maps.

As I have been hampered all my life by slow and clumsy handwriting, my ability to write did not match my ability to read or count or learn by rote, so perhaps for that reason I was not allowed to skip a class and did not sit the qualifying examination until I was thirteen years of age. We were among the last generation of pupils who were taught the art of writing not in exercise books but on slates. Each of us went to school equipped with a slate-pencil and a piece of rag for cleaning our slates. Girls from good homes with careful mothers would have in their school bag a piece of damp sponge to clean their slate, but we careless boys would use either a piece of rag or, occasionally, the sleeve of our jersey or jacket and would wet the slate by spitting on it when the teacher was not looking. A slate-pencil of poor quality or one with even a slight defect could make against the slate a horrible squeak which set the teeth on edge. At each major holiday period we were instructed to take our slates home and scrub the wooden frame until the wood was almost white.

The school was furnished with long desks which could seat up to eight pupils. The seat was a continuous bench which, as I recall, had no back-rest and was attached to the long desk by a cast-iron frame. The desks had a uniform slope, except for a few inches at the top which were flat and fitted with brass-covered inkwells and grooves for slate-pencils or pens. Beneath the sloping desk was a shelf for school bags and books. The only other furnishings were a high desk and chair for the teacher, a blackboard and a cupboard for books paper and handicraft materials. There was no musical instrument, not even a piano. The only item of furniture in the school which really attracted my interest was in the headmaster's classroom: a glass-fronted bookcase in dark wood which contained a good selection of books, most of them new to me. I was led to understand that this was a gift from a wealthy philanthropist. Although I cannot recall ever being encouraged by the headmaster to take any of these books home, or even to read them in school, I snatched opportunities, when I had finished my sums or exercises more speedily than some of my classmates, to read a few of them and so was introduced to the wonderful world of *Pilgrim's Progress Robinson Crusoe, Kidnapped, Lorna Doone* and tales by such writers as Fennimore Cooper and R M Ballantyne. Dickens and Scott were too dull for me at that early stage, although I did manage to enjoy *Ivanhoe* after wading through the first few chapters. Such reading, of course, belonged to the later years in the elementary school when I was under the rule of the headmaster.

In the lower classroom, where the headmaster's wife was in charge of the children from five up to about nine years of age, most of her time and energy were devoted to instilling into pupils of a wide range of ability the elements of reading, writing and arithmetic. A few of the pupils were so limited in ability that it must have been a depressing and almost impossible task, but no mercy was shown to the dull and backward who had a very miserable life in our school. Fortunately for me I was always well ahead of the pack in reading and arithmetic; my problem lay in clumsy hands either for handwriting or for handicraft. Apart from handwriting, the first hand skill which every pupil, boy and girl, was required to learn was how to knit. Every child in the classroom had to learn at least how to knit a woollen scarf, while the more skilled reached the stage, before the age of nine, of completing a pair of socks including the complex operation of turning the heel and finishing off the toe. I never reached that advanced stage, but knitted a scarf which grew longer and longer until it trailed on the floor when I had to bring it to the teacher's desk for occasional scrutiny, and that despite the fact that she repeatedly ripped many inches off the scarf when she discovered some mistake in the knitting. The final humiliation occurred when I took it home and my elder sister ripped it all out and used the wool for darning socks and pullovers. What a waste of effort!

For our teacher knitting must have been a favourite pastime, as I recall that she always had in the classroom a complex piece of knitting which she took up whenever the pupils were engaged in written work and she was relieved of oral teaching. The knitting was usually done on long, steel knitting needles. When the pupils were busy with written work she would walk behind the long benches, carrying the piece of knitting, and look over the pupils' shoulders. If anything about the writing displeased her, she would finish a row of knitting and then, with no warning, use the free needle to rap the guilty pupil hard on the knuckles. It was very painful. As I was a highly-strung child I got to the stage of freezing up and having writer's cramp whenever she paused behind me. That neurotic spasm became so automatic that it has lasted and embarrassed me all my life. In later life when I had many letters to sign, I had to warn my staff never to stand close to me or look on while I was writing. Occasionally I have been in real trouble when I have had to sign many documents in front of witnesses and my hand seized up.

Perhaps my hypersensitive temperament was to blame, but I must admit that I seldom enjoyed the hours which I spent in the classroom, under either the headmaster or his wife, although both were hard-working and efficient teachers within the limits of the narrow curriculum which was offered in the school. Of fun and humour and·laughter in these classrooms I can recall not a trace. Of harsh discipline and corporal punishment by the headmaster I can recall almost daily incidents, although I was seldom the victim of them. As I grew older it became increasingly obvious to me that a few pupils were simply incapable of understanding or completing correctly the exercises and calculations which I found well within my grasp. Written homework was often incorrect or incomplete; other homework which entailed rote learning of poems, hymns, psalms, the shorter catechism, multiplication tables or spelling lists could not be reproduced without errors or failures; new concepts and problems were beyond their understanding. Even at that early age I felt that what they needed was sympathy and help and demands on their limited ability which did not condemn them to perpetual failure; what they got was ill-temper, abuse, sarcasm and repeated strokes with the leather tawse. If as a result of pain or fear they drew away their hand, they were apt to receive strokes of the strap on their bare legs. Many a time I felt sad and sorry for them. At that time in rural communities it was not the done thing for parents to intervene between headmaster and pupil, and to my knowledge the parents of at least some of these pupils were in their social position and mentality as limited as their children. What they all needed but did not receive was help and understanding; on the other hand such parents could probably earn a better living in a rural community than in a town.

Our headmaster was a man of robust constitution who, during my years under his charge, was only once for some weeks absent because of illness. During that period the school had as locum a retired headmaster of whom I would probably have no clear recollection except for one thing: he was very fond of singing. In course of his short stay as headmaster he taught us, without accompaniment, to sing a number of Scots songs, such as *Afton Water, The Lea Rig, The Auld Hoose, Bonnie Strathyre* and the one about the wee boy gazing into the lowes of the open fire and *Biggin Castles in the Air*; songs which I enjoyed immensely and tunes which I still hum occasionally when I am in the mood. The singing of these Scots songs and the occasional reading of books from the bookcase are among the few really happy memories that remain with me from the classrooms of the elementary school.

Outside the classroom I had many interesting experiences and retain many pleasant memories of our rural school. The school lavatories belonged to the Victorian era as clearly as did the classroom desks and benches, the slates and the slate-pencils. Both boys and girls had dry closets; on the boys' side there was also a urinal with high walls. One of the claims to be a leader among the older boys, some of whom were nearing fourteen, was the ability to pee over the high wall of the urinal. It was a feat far beyond the ability of most of us who were under the age of twelve. At the opposite end of the playground the ground level was more than five feet higher than the level of the roadway outside the school and, as the playground wall was about five feet high, the drop from the top of the wall to the road was over ten feet. A second claim to leadership and manliness was the ability to hang from the wall by the fingertips and drop on to the road without injury. All that was required to succeed in this was a fair measure of confidence and relaxation, yet it was surprising how many of the senior boys re fused the challenge.

The ball games which we played were much the same as the games of today; some other games which we played I have not seen children play in the past generation. We played with girds or hoops, which were metal rings about the size of a bicycle wheel driven along by a stout wire rod with a hook on the end; we whipped wooden tops with the fag-end of a rope; we played games with marbles; we played quoits with horse shoes; we played rounders with a soft ball and we played cat's cradle with a loop of string. The girls also had a variety of games which seemed to change with the seasons: games with skipping ropes, soft balls, hop scotch and jacks (or chacks) in addition to some which they played in common with the boys.

As there were no school meals during my years at school, the general custom for those who lived some distance away from school was to bring sandwiches, or pieces as we called them, to serve for the midday meal. This was also the custom in our family while our mother was there to care for us, but after mother's death we had to rely much more on each other to get ready for school and quite often the preparation of sandwiches was forgotten until too late. On these occasions the eldest child at school was given one shilling (5p) wherewith to buy biscuits at the village shop. As the village shop was half a mile beyond the school, one of the brothers had to trot about a mile at the beginning of the midday interval to buy biscuits for the family lunch. The biscuits had, of course, to be eaten dry but they seemed to satisfy us, especially when the shop had a good supply of broken biscuits which were sold cheaply.

The long morning walk to school was tedious and, in stormy, snowy or frosty weather could be not merely tedious but quite trying, for there was no time for loitering as the headmaster would accept no excuse if any pupil arrived late for school. The two-mile walk home, by comparison, could at most seasons be interesting and sometimes could be fun. For me the most interesting season was the time when the birds were nesting, as it was a matter of pride to discover every nest built in the hedges, dykes and ditches along both sides of the road between home and school. As Kintyre with its mild climate and, at that time, freedom from motor vehicles and pesticides was a haven for birds, there was quite a variety of nests to be found; and learning where to look, what to look for and to recognise the various kinds of nests and the different sizes, shapes and colours of eggs without disturbing the birds was self-education of the best type and fascinating compared with anything taught at school. In the same way we did our best to find the nests of every kind of bird which nested in the ploughed fields or the pasture or the boundary hedges and ditches or the hill land of the farm. These included most of the birds such as blackbirds, finches, linnets, robins, tits, thrushes, wagtails, wrens and yellowhammers which nested in hedges, dykes and ditches by the roadside and additional birds which nested on the farm, including corncrakes and partridges in the hayfield, peewits in the stubble and ploughed land, curlews, grouse, greyhens, larks, moor linnets, pheasants, snipe and woodcock on the hill ground; while around the farm steading were the nests of house-martins, sparrows, starlings and swallows. Of all these the snipe's nest was often the most difficult to find. Only once was I fortunate enough to find a cuckoo's egg in a linnet's nest.

By the seashore there was another range of nests to be found in the sand dunes, in the shoals of gravel and seaweed and on the cliffs. Of equal interest was the variety of pebbles and seashells and also the variety of small living creatures to be found in rock pools. These were the kinds of activities and fields of knowledge which enriched the life of children growing up in the countryside but which had no place in our formal education. They were not so much taught as absorbed from our everyday living, from parents and older members of the family, from kindly and interested people in the community and from the pals with whom we argued and fought and played and spent our leisure time.

Chapter 3
The Transport Revolution

DURING MY ELEMENTARY school days none of the roads in the district was surfaced with tar-macadam or asphalt; the road surface was what was known as water-bound, which I suppose was the original macadam surface. As none of the local quarries had a mechanical stone-crusher, all the stone used for roadmaking and surfacing had to be broken by hand into the required sizes. At intervals along the roadside a lay-by was formed and filled with loads of stone which had been blasted in the quarries. Men who were known as stone-knappers were employed to break the larger stones down into the sizes needed for making or repairing road surfaces. Each of these men had a series of hammers ranging in weight from seven-pound to one-pound hammers, and they acquired skill at breaking the large stones along lines of cleavage until the smallest stones would go through a half-inch riddle. Many a chat we had with these men on the way home from school, when my elder brothers would be given a chance to use the hammers and try their hand at stone knapping.

After the 1914-18 war, when motor vehicles replaced the horse-drawn carts and buggies, the water-bound road surfaces could not stand up to the wear and tear and had to be replaced with tar-macadam. About the same time mechanical stone-crushing machinery was installed in our local quarries and our friends the stone-knappers became redundant. In the water-bound road surface the stones of graded size were actually bound with clay or sand, filtered by water between the stones and made solid by a heavy steam-driven road roller. While such roads would stand up for years to horse-drawn traffic, they were soon pitted with potholes by the greater speed and weight of buses, cars and trucks.

For me the old roads had one advantage: some of the clay and sand, washed out by heavy rain, formed a soft path on each verge of the road. In summer all the children from poorer homes came to school in bare feet and had no footwear until the colder weather of Autumn. While my family went to school in boots which we called tackety boots, we loved to discard our boots and run barefoot around the farm in hot weather. Sometimes the temptation to take off our boots when coming home from school in warm summer days was too strong to resist. When feet were bare it was a great comfort to walk along the mud path by the roadside rather than on the rough stones of the road surface. From an early age I enjoyed running and often trotted, with bare feet and boots tied to the school bag, all the way home from school. Many a time a scolding awaited me when I arrived home with mud spattered up my legs and back.

In 1916, when I was four years old, I first saw a motor vehicle pass our farm and this, to my knowledge, was the first motor vehicle owned by a member of our community. It was not a motor car but an open truck owned by a member of the well-known Coats family of Paisley who had an estate in our parish. On this vehicle two of the wheels were fitted with solid rubber tyres while the other two had pneumatic tyres. Shortly thereafter the first motor cars arrived in the parish, and soon the first tractors were to be seen in the fields. Within a very few years the mighty revolution in motive power and transport was accepted by everyone, and our concept of time and distance had to be radically revised, as what we conceived to be a day's journey on foot or by cart could be completed in less than an hour by motor car, while a load which took a whole day to transport by horse and cart could be transported in an hour by motor truck. In rural areas the coming of the motor omnibus (or 'bus) was equally important, especially for those families who could not afford a motor car, for travel by bus was fast, relatively inexpensive and liberated people who previously had rarely been able to travel any great distance from home. Regular bus transport provided young people with new opportunities to travel to work, and also provided new freedom, for women in particular, to travel independently to town for shopping and recreation. In the days of the horse and buggy wives were rarely seen travelling with their husbands to town or market, except on the occasions when fairs or agricultural shows were held. To those women who lived in rural areas the motor bus became the great social liberator.

The first journey by bus which I can recall carried some of my brothers and me from Campbeltown to Grandma Young's farm of Cleongart for our summer holiday. That bus, like the first truck which I had seen, was fitted with two solid rubber tyres and two pneumatic tyres and while it had a canvas cover it had no windscreen. As the road had not yet been surfaced with tar macadam, the ride on solid rubber tyres was very bumpy and, although the bus did not exceed twenty miles per hour, I recall feeling quite queasy by the end of the twelve mile journey, so my first experience of motor transport was not of the happiest. The bus driver wore a heavy waterproof coat and peaked cap to repel the rain. The motor bus on which I travelled was a recent replacement for the stage coach which had run between Campbeltown and Tarbert and which, for many years had been owned and driven by one of my father's uncles. This was the stage coach on which my father had travelled during his last few years in school.

Although I had not seen a motor vehicle, except in pictures, before 1916 I had become quite accustomed to seeing a much larger form of transport, namely airships, since soon after the outbreak of war in 1914. The seaports on the River Clyde were still among the world's great centres of shipping, and in the Firth of Clyde were formed the convoys of merchant ships which sailed through the North Channel between Kintyre and northern Ireland, surrounded by warships and guarded overhead by huge airships which flew slowly at the speed of the convoy, or occasionally travelled ahead of the convoy to watch for signs of enemy ships or, more probably, enemy submarines. For four years we were privileged to watch those great convoys of ships as they steamed outwards and homewards through the North Channel at all seasons and in all weathers, many of them torpedoed and sunk on the high seas with huge loss of men and materials, but still battling to maintain a precarious lifeline for the people of the country at war. Even in 1918 I was still too young to understand fully the deprivation, loss and sorrow which the war had brought to many families and, being fortunate to live on a farm, my family probably suffered much less from rationing and shortage of food than those who lived in towns and cities. Yet I still recall some of the shortages, especially of sugar and flour for baking girdle scones which, in normal times, were baked every day in the farm kitchen, and I recall some of the horror stories of rat and mouse excrement and occasionally rats' legs being found in flour, and of jam being made mainly of turnips. I can certainly recall that home-made jam was a great treat compared with the inferior variety bought in the grocer's shop. Strangely enough I carry no memory of the actual ending of the war in 1918, save the memory of some young men who had been fortunate enough to survive the war but seemed to have no wish to talk about what they had endured, when they again settled down to work on the family farm.

Chapter 4
Life on the Farm

THE LOYALTY OF MY father to his farm was one of the few matters on which he and I, when I had grown up, strongly disagreed. The farm was, in my view, too small to be a good economic farming unit. It comprised about eighty acres of indifferent arable land and about seventy acres of hill ground, partly heather-covered and partly rough pasture, The arable land was divided into about a dozen small fields, of which half were reasonably flat with a fair depth of soil; the other half-dozen fields were on a variable incline with rather thin, shallow soil which had to be heavily manured to maintain its fertility. While the climate was mild, the annual rainfall was usually excessive and the weather was often dull, with too few hours of sunshine to compensate for the annual rainfall. In short it was a good climate for pasture but not for the cultivation and harvesting of crops. Because of the relatively wet climate and the inability of the subsoil to absorb the rain, field drains were commonly dug at five-yard intervals, and almost every field had an open boundary ditch to carry away surplus water and help to prevent flooding. Apart from the smallness of the farm, it seemed to me that the worst aspect of farming in Kintyre was the frequency with which farmers were struggling against the weather instead of cooperating with it, and the next worst aspect was the distance from the main markets, especially in the days before motor transport arrived on the scene.

The arable land was usually managed on an eight-year rotation, which involved three years under the plough and five years in grass. When the pasture land was ploughed it was referred to as 'lea', and the crop grown on lea was usually oats or barley.

In the second year of cultivation the crop was usually one which helped to clean the ground, such as turnips, potatoes or forage kale. For a few years farmers were encouraged to grow sugar-beet but the climate and the cost of transport proved too much of a deterrent for most of the farms in the district. In the third year of cultivation, after the soil cleansing crop, barley or oats or, occasionally, a crop of beans was grown. After sowing the field was rolled with a heavy roller, then grass seed was sown and lightly harrowed in to produce pasture for the next five years. After the first grain crop the ground was referred to as 'stubble' and after the cleansing crop was gathered the ground was generally called 'redland'.

As the greater part of the farm land at any time was under pasture, the most important feature of the farm was not the growing of crops but the keeping and management of livestock. On our farm, as on most of the farms in the district, by far the most important unit of livestock was the herd of milk cows. Most of the farmers in the district would regard their farm as a dairy farm, although the typical holding in the area was a mixed farm in which the dairy herd was the most important element. Because our farm was relatively small and intensive methods of farming were not practised, the dairy herd comprised only between twenty and twenty-four milk cows. As the farm during my childhood had no milking machine, the cows were milked by hand morning and evening. Except for the small amount required for family use, or to feed young calves, the milk was processed into large Dunlop cheeses for most of the year, and into smaller stilton-shaped cheeses when the cows produced less milk as they approached calving in the Spring.

In addition to the dairy herd the farm always kept some pigs, some young cattle, some hens and, occasionally, a small flock of sheep. By arrangement with the Factor of the Argyll Estate, my father always provided pasture during the Winter for about a hundred ewe lambs that were born on one of the hill farms near the Mull of Kintyre which were managed by shepherds in the Duke's employment. These upland farms were among the few that were not let to tenant farmers but were let in the shooting season to sportsmen who generally had parties of guests for grouse, partridge and pheasant shooting. It was found by experience that the lambs or hoggets from these upland farms survived and thrived better if they spent their first winter season on low ground. From the training which he had received in Cleongart in his youth my father was skilled in handling sheep, and he devoted much time and care to looking after the young sheep during the winter. For all that care and the use of the pasture, supplemented by loads of turnips when the ground was covered with snow, my father received five shillings (25p) for each hogget that survived the winter. That small sum was regarded as a useful addition to the income of the farm.

Special mention must be made of the Clydesdale horses who were essential to the working of the farm and who supplied the energy which now comes from tractors, trucks and other machinery driven by electric power or by internal combustion engines. To the male farm workers, both the hired men and my grown- up brothers, the stable was the hub of the farm. There they met before and after every meal to feed and groom the horses and to harness and unharness them before and after every working shift; there they formed a male enclave which the women of the household rarely penetrated; there they spent much of their leisure time, sitting on the corn kist or on bales of hay or straw; there they could indulge in gossip, discussion, argument, talk too coarse for the ears of women, boasting of sexual prowess and occasional practical jokes. There at weekends men from other farms would sometimes join them for a session of talk, stories, music and song. The farm usually kept two pairs of Clydesdale mares and a gelding for heavy carting and also for replacing a mare which was due to give birth to a foal. In addition to the teams of Clydesdale horses every farm kept a pony for drawing a dog-cart or buggy, which was the farmer's mode of transport to market and the family's transport to church or social outings. During my childhood the pony on our farm was a little grey cob which we yoked to a buggy, and father was pestered by all the children, as they grew up, to be allowed to drive the pony in the buggy.

Every year an endeavour was made, not always with success, to have one of the mares in foal. A feature of country life at that time was the travelling stallion which was led around the district from farm to farm by his groom for the express purpose of serving or covering the mares judged by the farmers to be most suited for breeding in that particular season. At the beginning of a season of travelling a Clydesdale Stallion in top fettle was a magnificent animal, fed and groomed to perfection throughout the winter, with powerful shoulders and haunches, proudly curved neck, a gleaming coat, long silky hair on mane and lower limbs, eyes flashing in a shapely head and prancing along the road as if he were in charge of his groom instead of the groom being in control of him. By the end of a long season he was much quieter and sometimes seemed to be exhausted by his daily travels and the number of mares he had covered. Most of the stallions had gained prizes at national shows as outstanding representatives of their breed, and some earned a national reputation for the quality of the foals which they sired, as from time to time they moved to a different district until they became known throughout most of the country.

The grooms who looked after the stallions were usually outgoing characters, welcomed by the men of the farms for the gossip which they carried and the ribald stories which they told, and occasionally welcomed by the younger maidservants for being as lively as the stallion which they led. The serving or covering of a mare at a farm was a ceremony in which only the men of the farm were supposed to be interested but it was impracticable to quell the curiosity of the younger males, who were generally looking round the corner of the farm steading, for though they had seen the bull and the boar and the ram in action every year, a Clydesdale stallion in action was a truly impressive sight. The groom in charge of the stallion usually ignored the boys peering round the corner, but I recall that on one occasion he blasted with foul language a young maidservant whose curiosity had brought her to peer through one of the windows of the byre which faced on to the farm close. Quite often a mare had to be covered more than once in a season, and even then there was no certainty that she would produce a foal. When the time came for a foal to be born there was obvious concern among the men of the farm, especially if a young mare was carrying her first foal, for a difficult birth seemed to be more common among horses than among cattle, and loss of either the mother or the foal was a serious loss to the farm. A young foal was a great attraction to everyone on the farm whether in the loosebox after its birth or in the field suckling and playing round its mother.

As a foal grew up the first stage in its training to become a workhorse was to halter it as gently as possible and let it become accustomed to being led on a rope halter. When the young horse was about ready for work the halter was replaced by a bridle and bit, the latter an unwelcome adjunct which the animal did all it could to reject, and I must admit that my sympathy always lay with the young horse, for the bit was the ultimate symbol of subjection and marked the end of its youth and joyous freedom. The next stage was to accustom the horse to bearing a load, and that was where we younger boys had an active part to play, for usually one of us was gently eased on to the horse's back where we were held by one of the men while another held the bridle rope. It was expected that the boy would be thrown off by the horse and caught by one of the men a few times before the young animal grew accustomed to the load and moved quietly under the control of the bridle and bit. When the horse had learned to accept the bit in its mouth and a load on its back, it soon grew accustomed to the weight of a saddle and the tightening of a girth. It was then ready to be yoked and trained to work as one of a pair in pulling a plough and as one of three in pulling a binder.

Chapter 5
To be a Farmer's Boy

AFTER MY MOTHER DIED in 1917, leaving her family for ever bereft of the love and care which only she could give, my father did his best in the limited time he could spare to look after the upbringing of his seven children, including my sister Jean who had not yet reached her second birthday. For some time one of my aunts from Cleongart lived with us and kept house, but she was not prepared to carry the burden of work in byre and dairy which my mother had borne and she soon returned home to Cleongart. From then on my father had to rely wholly on hired maids to do the housekeeping, the milking, the feeding of livestock and the making of cheese and butter in the dairy. Fortunately for my father and the children the senior housemaid, who had been with us for several years had become very attached to the family and especially to baby Jean; so she took over the burden of the byre and dairy, along with a younger girl who was hired to do the housework and help with the milking. My eldest brother, John, had been given exemption from attendance at school and, while still under the age of fourteen, became a full-time farm worker. The next brother, Donald, was required to busy himself after school and at weekends in feeding cattle and pigs, milking cows and cleaning out the byre and piggery.

The younger children were all given tasks to do around the farm steading and were required to help, up to the limit of their ability and strength, in the seasonal work of the farm. I recall that from the age of six one of my daily jobs was to break with a hammer the large lumps of coal which were brought by the cart-load from the local coalpit at Drumlemble, then fill the broken coal into buckets ready to be carried by one of my older brothers into the dairy to heat the water boiler, and also into the coal-cupboard off the kitchen to fuel the kitchen range. On the kitchen range, with its side oven, the family meals were cooked and the family baking was fired, while the heating of the kitchen also depended on maintaining a good fire in the range. This was very important in cold, wintry weather, for the kitchen was the main family living room and dining room; the lounge was used only on special occasions when visitors were present or friends had been invited to spend the evening.

Although the coal produced from the pit at Drumlemble was not of the highest quality and left a large residue of grey ash in the grate, it cost about one pound per ton at the pit-head and its price advantage against coal shipped into the district created a constant demand for it. A more indirect advantage was that the pit justified the building and running of one of the shortest narrow-gauge railways in Britain: the railway from the pier in Campbeltown via Drumlemble to Machrihanish, a total distance of about five miles. For most of its relatively short life the little railway carried goods trains and passenger trains at a modest speed of not more than thirty miles an hour and was well patronised prior to the motor era. When local coal mining declined and buses as well as private cars grew in numbers, the little railway became increasingly uneconomic and, sadly, had to be closed down. If it were still running today it might possibly have paid its way as a tourist attraction.

In addition to the specified tasks which we children had to perform around the farm steading, and which increased with age and strength, we were also required to help from an early age with the seasonal work of the farm as it continued and varied throughout the year. While school was in session we could help only in the evenings and at weekends, but during school holidays we increasingly became, as we grew older, almost full-time farm workers. One of the hardest and most unpleasant tasks, the singling or thinning of turnips, usually coincided with the beginning of the summer holidays. On our farm as on most of the farms in the district, the turnip crop was the main crop grown in the second year of cultivation for two reasons: turnips were good for feeding livestock and the crop was also good for cleaning the land and keeping weeds in check. Because of the relatively wet climate and the nature of the soil, the singling of turnips on our farm was not done by the hoe but by hand. We prepared for the work by binding round our legs jute sacks which had been suitably folded to protect our knees. The turnip seed was sown by a horse-drawn implement which sowed two drills at a time. When the young turnip plants were between two and three inches high, another horse-drawn machine equipped with four cutting discs and called a 'scarifier' removed some of the soil from two drills at a time, and left a ridge a few inches wide on which the young plants mixed with weeds were growing. We singled or thinned the turnips by crawling along on our knees between two drills and by removing with our hands the ridge of soil along with the weeds and surplus turnip seedlings, leaving only one plant at intervals of about nine inches.

For us children the thinning of turnips was a tiresome and thoroughly disagreeable task, partly because of the wear and tear on our knees but even more by the wear and tear on our hands. The damage to our hands was aggravated by the fact that the singling of turnips took place at the beginning of the school holidays when our hands were soft and the skin easily damaged. Strange as it may seem, this was one of the few tasks on the farm which we found easier when the weather was wet or at least damp, because the cool, soft soil did less damage to our hands and knees, even though by the end of the day the sacks which protected our knees were heavy with mud or 'glaur' as we called it. During a spell of dry sunny weather, which often occurred in June, several days spent crawling on the rough, hot earth and tearing at the hard drills with soft hands became a prolonged torture, as knees grew red and tender and the skin was literally worn off our fingers till they bled.

However much I suffered at singling turnips it was one of the many times throughout the year when I had to watch with admiration the example set by my father. Because his right knee was permanently locked he was compelled when singling turnips to crawl along the drill on his left knee, which took almost all his weight, while his right leg was stretched across the ridge of turnips which he was actually singling. Despite that immense handicap, his hands and arms were so powerful that he worked faster than any of his family or his hired men, and some time later, when the turnips had grown larger, we could always point to the drills which father had singled because of his remarkable skill in selecting the strongest plants to produce the fastest growth and the best crop. Some weeks after the turnips were singled by hand, we went over the whole field again with hoes to remove any weeds which had been left to grow, and thus the ground was cleansed for the remainder of the growing season.

It was a great relief, after the purgatory of thinning turnips, to turn to the cleaner and more pleasant task of making hay, even though the later stages of haymaking could test young muscles to the utmost. On our small farm my father usually planned to grow hay on one field of five or six acres, partly because the high rainfall made haymaking chancy and partly because most of the grassland was required as pasture for the milk cows and other livestock. The pasture intended for hay was generously manured in the Spring to ensure fast growth and a heavy crop. Early in July, if the weather forecast was favourable, the hay was cut by reaper drawn by two horses, and the cut hay lay in swathes for several days before it was turned over by hand rakes to be thoroughly dried. All too often, because of unsettled weather, the hay was soaked before it was fit to be built into coles and, during a wet season, it had to be turned several times in the swathe. When sufficiently weathered and dry the hay was raked into large piles and built up in the hayfield into what we called ricks, which were of a size that could be loaded on to a farm cart. There the hay lay for some weeks until it had matured enough to be ready for stacking.

There was one aspect of haymaking which I did not enjoy although I was not then aware, nor do I believe that most people were aware, of the disastrous effect it would have on one of our favourite birds. When cutting hay by reaper it was common practice to cut round the boundaries of the field, and to continue cutting all four sides of the crop until only a thin strip was left in the centre of the field to be cut as the final swathe. The catastrophe was due to the fact that corncrakes chose hayfields as their favourite nesting place and, when the hay was cut, either the mother bird was brooding eggs which were due to hatch, or the eggs had already been hatched and the parent birds were guarding the baby birds among the hay. If the mother was brooding eggs she would sit tight until mangled by the swiftly moving blades of the reaper knife; if the parent birds were guarding their young the fledglings would freeze to the ground while the parents, all too often, stood guard until their legs were sliced off by the reaper blades. In either event a family of corncrakes perished, and the slaughter was repeated annually in hay-meadows throughout the countryside. It was a sight which I loathed to see but, because of the secretive habits of the birds, could do little to prevent. When I was young the corncrakes in our district were as numerous as the cuckoos, and their harsh calls could be heard from every meadow until one fell asleep at night. How callous and thoughtless we were not to realise that the annual slaughter must end in the virtual extinction of the bird that was continually heard but rarely seen until mangled by the sharp blades of the reaper knife.

At few of the smaller farms in my youth was hay stored in a hayshed, for the simple reason that most small farms did not possess a hayshed, and the tenant farmers could not persuade their landowner to have one built. The common practice was to cart the hay from the field to the stackyard and build it into stacks, which were then thatched and roped until the hay was needed for winter feed. The carting and stacking of hay in our district was one of those tasks which were most efficiently done by the cooperation of neighbouring farmers and their staffs. The main reason for the cooperative effort, which showed farmers and farm workers at their best, was a rick-lifter of a type which I have not seen elsewhere. The rick-lifter was a tripod mounted on wheels, with stout wooden legs up to thirty feet in length and fitted at the apex with a pulley and wire rope to which were attached three chains with strong metal forks for inserting under the base of a hayrick. The other end of the wire rope ran from the pulley block down metal hoops to the foot of one leg of the tripod, where it was attached to a swingle-tree. When erected in a hayfield the tripod was pulled along by a horse until settled over a hayrick; the three steel forks were inserted under the rick and when the horse was led away from the tripod it operated the pulley mechanism to lift the rick into the air. When the base of the rick reached a sufficient height a farm cart was backed under it; the horse controlling the wire rope was then backed until the rick rested securely on the cart and the steel forks were withdrawn. When the laden cart moved off to the stackyard, the rick-lifter was towed by the horse to the next rick and the operation of raising the rick and loading the next cart was repeated. The whole process was so simple and quick that up to six or more carts could be kept busy transporting ricks from the field to the stackyard, where two stacks could be built at the same time.

Depending upon the distance from the hayfield to the stackyard, up to fifteen men could be kept busy on this cooperative task, and could usually complete the carting and stacking of the hay in one day. The process was repeated at each of the farms which joined in the cooperative venture and so investment in only one expensive rick-lifter was required. We children enjoyed the stacking of the hay because so much banter went on among the men; food and drink were served in abundance; teasing and laughter greeted the women who served the food, and the mood was invariably cheerful and good-natured as befitted a gathering of neighbours.

When the weather was not suitable for haymaking, the older children in our family were sent out with scythes to cut down weeds such as thistles, dockens and ragwort which had grown in the pasture fields and along the sides of boundary ditches. Although my father was insistent that no weeds be allowed to grow until they had cast their seed and thus produce another crop of weeds, the objective was never quite achieved; the pasture fields were kept clean and no doubt the noxious weeds were kept from multiplying as fast as they otherwise would have done, but every year produced a fresh crop of weeds which had to be cut. The use of the scythe to cut weeds made each of us children familiar and practised in swinging a scythe when we became old enough to use it at harvest time. We also gained practice at a fairly early age in the art of sharpening the blade of a scythe with a whetstone, an essential skill which could result in a deeply cut hand if it were not practised with due care. Very few boys grew up on a farm without at some time suffering a cut on a scythe blade and, when it did occur, if it was self-inflicted and due to carelessness, the victim received very little sympathy. Gaining skill at various tasks on a farm was not always easy or free from pain and, indeed, one of the lessons all of us had to learn was how to bear pain stoically and not make a fuss about it.

As our farm only occasionally pastured a small flock of sheep, apart from the hoggets from a hill sheep farm which my father pastured during the winter months, it was not often that we children had an opportunity to take part in another of the main tasks which farmers and shepherds carried out annually as a cooperative venture: that was the shearing and dipping of the flock. On a hill farm the lambing and the shearing were the two biggest tasks of the year. As the bulk of the flocks in our district were blackface ewes acclimatised or hefted on the hill land where they were born, the shearing took place rather later in the summer than with flocks shepherded on lowland farms. If wool was not to suffer damage through heating in the woolsack, sheep had to be clipped when the wool was dry, and the ideal conditions were when the fleece to be shorn was slightly raised by the new wool beginning to grow underneath. When season and weather were right for sheepshearing the whole flock, including the lambs, was gathered and driven in early morning from the hill to the pens (or fanks as they were known locally) where the shearing was organised. In order to ensure that only one gathering of the flock was needed for shearing the whole stock, several farms usually worked together at a shearing, which at its best could become a notable social occasion as well as a long day of skilled and tiring work.

When I was a child mechanical equipment for shearing sheep had not yet been adopted on our local sheep farms, and the clipping was all done with hand shears, which demanded skill and patience as well as ensuring that shepherds developed a strength of hand and arm that matched the strength of their legs. A long day spent at hand-shearing sheep was a real test of strength, endurance and skill in which, as in other arts, some shepherds excelled their fellows, and occasionally among the younger men there was an element of rivalry. The older and more experienced shepherds had acquired the art of pacing themselves to ensure that they lasted the whole day without becoming exhausted. They found time to exchange gossip, tales and repartee and, as shepherds were often men of considerable ability who found satisfaction and self-reliance in the rather lonely life of shepherding, the repartee was sometimes of a high order and flowed as freely as the drinks with which they quenched their thirst. Some of the most humorous and fluent talk to which I have been privileged to listen took place among the experienced shepherds at a sheep shearing.

We children were not welcomed at a sheep shearing unless we were willing to help in whatever way we could: running errands, handing round food and drink, carrying shorn fleeces to the huge woolsack in which the wool was packed by two men, one throwing the fleeces up into the sack which hung on a tall wooden frame, and the other inside the sack treading the fleeces underfoot until the sack was fully and tightly packed; then as we grew older, helping to draw the sheep from the fanks to the benches where the shearers worked, often with their shirts damp and the sweat dripping from their faces. If a sheep was unusually strong and stubborn it would sometimes take two of us, each holding on to a horn, to drag it from the fanks to the shearers. As a child I often wondered by what kind of magic a shepherd would take hold of a sheep which two of us could barely manage, swing it over on to its back, turn its head to one side and proceed to shear it while it lay as peacefully as if it enjoyed the whole operation. It seemed to me that an experienced shepherd had an empathy with his sheep as he had with his sheepdogs, and as an experienced ploughman had with his team of horses.

On our farm the next main task after the stacking of the hay was the grain harvest, which was a pleasure in a dry season but, more often in our wet, uncertain climate, could be a long and tedious business. As my father liked to keep the fields well fertilised in order to get the biggest possible crop, large areas of the crop were all too often laid and tangled by heavy rain, and sometimes flattened to the ground for so long that the heads of corn had begun to sprout with new growth. It sometimes occurred to me that it would have been preferable to aim at a lighter crop of grain which could stand up to the weather and be harvested with less labour and less waste. Barley straw being stronger than oat straw, barley was less likely to be flattened by rain, but that to us was only minor relief as the major grain crop on our farm was oats, with barley or beans an occasional crop. When I was a child the binder had already replaced the reaper on larger farms, but in the years of depression in agriculture which blighted the nineteen-twenties, having lost the invaluable help of my mother and having to bear the cost and responsibility of raising a large, young family, my father could not afford to invest in a binder. He still depended on the reaper and the scythe to cut the grain crop. As every effort had to be made to avoid waste, even if it entailed extra labour, the first few days of harvesting were usually done with the scythe rather than with the reaper. The initial phase was the scything of what we called 'roads' right round the boundary or end rig of the field of grain, the road being the width of one sweep of the scythe, which just provided room for two horses yoked to the reaper to walk abreast witout treading down any of the crop. After cutting the roads the next step was to cut with the scythe any patches of the field where the crop was too badly flattened by wind and rain to be cut effectively by the reaper. The corn cut by making the roads and scything the tangled areas had, of course, to be bundled, bound into sheaves and carried to the side of the field to give free passage to the reaper.

Whereas for cutting hay the reaper required only a driver, for cutting a grain crop a partnership of two was necessary: a driver and a more highly skilled person to operate the mechanism which ensured that sheaves of oats, barley or beans would be well-shaped and uniform in size. Because of the skill which he had built up over the years my father always operated the sheaving mechanism or rack, and to that end he had bought a reaper with the cutting bar on the left side, for the rack was operated by a foot lever which entailed keeping the leg straight and the rack raised while the sheaf was being formed, then bending the knee to lower the rack to the ground and thus allow the sheaf to be swept off the rack with a broad-bladed rake specially designed for the purpose. Although complex to describe, the formation of sheaves and the mechanism used appeared simple to the observer, but in practice the skill of the person in control of the sheaving mechanism made the difference between sheaves which were ragged in shape and uneven in size and sheaves which were neat in shape, easily handled and uniform in size. To excel at the task required a high degree of coordination and bodily rhythm and, as I have previously mentioned, my father tended to excel at operations which demanded these qualities. The special rake which was used in conjunction with the rack had a head almost as wide as the cutter bar of the reaper, long teeth and a spadelike handle set into the head of the rake at an angle of about forty five degrees. The rake had to be swung very accurately in a rhythmical sweep as soon as the rack was lowered to the ground, so that the sheaf could be swept off the rack without leaving any straw behind, and with the bottom of the sheaf neatly formed and ready to be gathered and bound by the harvesters following behind the reaper. Immediately the sheaf was swept off, the operator raised the rack by straightening his leg on the lever pedal and the next sheaf began to form.

The harvesters who followed the reaper usually included men, women and boys who worked in teams of three. The woman or child would draw from the sheaf a handful of straw, quickly divide it into two, take the two ends near the grain and, with a twist of the wrists, form a strap of straw which was placed on the ground. The second person was meantime gathering the sheaf into a neat bundle which was placed on the strap. The woman and child then moved on to the next sheaf to repeat the operation. The man bound the sheaf tightly with the strap of straw by binding one end round the other and then tucking the free end underneath the strap. He carried the sheaf on to the next sheaf which he bound in the same way and then placed the two sheaves a little way from the uncut grain. When four sheaves were gathered the man formed them into the beginning of a stook by leaning pairs of sheaves firmly together at an angle which was designed to secure stability and keep the grain off the ground. When the next cut was made by the reaper two or four more sheaves would be added to make a stook of six or eight sheaves which would stand up to the wind and permit the grain to dry. The stooks stood in the field until the grain and straw were thoroughly dried and then they were carted to the stackyard to be built into stacks.

The building of neat, trim stacks was one of the many farming operations in which every good farmer took pride. On our farm the stools on which the stacks were built were circular platforms about nine inches in height, made up of stones gathered from the fields. While the stools served to keep the base of the stacks dry, they provided easy access and shelter for mice and rats which found the stacks to be ideal as both a cosy home and a ready larder during the winter, so every stack had its population of rodents, which in turn attracted both owls and weasels. On some farms the stacks were built around a cone-shaped, hollow framework which introduced a measure of ventilation into the base of the stack, but that device was not used on our farm. The building of the corn stack was started by placing a few sheaves almost upright at the centre of the stool, then building rows of sheaves round the central core, each row overlapping the previous row until the ends of the circular row of sheaves reached the outer edge of the stool. The stack was then built up as a circular shape with an inner and an outer row of sheaves at each level, the sheaves being packed as tightly as the builder could manage, and the inner row overlapping the outer row with the heads of grain always towards the centre of the stack. A well-built stack did not rise vertically but sloped slightly outwards up to the eaves which could be twelve to fifteen feet high; then each row of sheaves was narrowed progressively to form a conical top which was finished off with a group of upstanding sheaves like a circular stook, bound together at the top to form a peak. The sloping top of the stack was later thatched with rushes and bound by circles of rope threaded through vertical ropes, which held the thatch in place and kept the stack watertight. Only the most violent of storms could disturb a stack which had been well-built, thatched and roped.

Out in the harvest field the carts were built up with sheaves by the drivers, whose task it was to ensure that the several rows of sheaves were so tightly and evenly built that no embarrassing slippage could take place on the journey from the field to the stackyard. If a load of sheaves capsized, as sometimes it did, the injury which the driver suffered by falling off the load was usually less painful than the teasing which went on for days afterwards, and did much to ensure greater care in future. Forking the sheaves all day from the stooks on to the farm carts was exhausting work, yet it was a task often assigned to women or to older children. Many an hour have I spent in my youth forking sheaves on to the carts in the harvest field, with sweat running down my back and dripping from my chin in warm weather, thirst quenched with draughts of sour buttermilk laced with a handful of oatmeal in the pitcher, and returning home in the evening dusk to devour a large supper and soon after strip off, sponge down and fall into bed, utterly worn out and with aching muscles, and sleep without stirring until roused in the morning to help clean the stable, curry the Clydesdale horses, then into breakfast with porridge and milk, home-cured bacon and eggs and out to the harvest field to repeat the effort of the previous day. That was the kind of work which, in the countryside of my youth, made many a boy into a man thirled to the life of the land, while it made others vow to seek for themselves an easier way of making a living. Although I became, almost by chance, one of the latter I have for the rest of my life looked back on those days of toil on the farm with a real measure of nostalgia. It was a life which bred good, hardy men who could stand up to all the rigours of life and who proved in times of war to have the physical resilience and mental toughness which characterised the Scottish soldier.

Later in my youth my father acquired a binder which was drawn by a team of three horses and which, though an irritating brute when it gave mechanical trouble, as it often did, served to speed up the cutting of the grain and freed us from the heavy labour of bunching and binding the sheaves which the binder did mechanically. It also relieved us in large measure from the worst plague of the harvest field: the continuous attacks by the hordes of midges which were at their worst around harvest time, and which swarmed over one's arms, face and neck when bending over to bunch and bind the sheaves which were cast from the reaper. As there was no way of escaping the midges which swarmed among the corn, we had to endure their bites for hours on end and I was fortunate that, however painful they were, my skin recovered quickly at the close of the day. The only operation behind the binder was stooking the sheaves, which kept one on the move and less liable to torture by midges. Looking back over the variety of work which I did as a youth on the farm, I think the height of my ambition was attained when my father allowed me to drive the binder in a field where the crop was not too badly tangled and lodged. To a young lad there was something infinitely satisfying in being in control of three massive Clydesdale horses yoked to a powerful machine which cut a clean swathe round a field of grain, swept the sward on to a moving conveyor, formed, bunched and bound each sheaf and with a click of the revolving fork cast the well-formed sheaf clear of the binder. I have never again achieved the same peak of satisfaction from driving a tractor, or a motor car, or even a battle tank in the 1939-45 war. Perhaps such peaks of satisfaction are among the privileges of youth.

After the grain harvest came the potato harvest which, much to my relief, was not of major importance on our farm since, in most years, potatoes were grown mainly for domestic use rather than for sale as a cash crop. In our damp climate the gathering of potatoes behind the mechanical digger, drawn by two horses, was no fun as it generally resulted only in a painful back. One facet of the potato crop merits special mention. Just as in his youth my father had spent many days in winter carting seaweed from the shore to spread on the land, so he continued to employ his sons and his hired men when the ground in winter was too wet for ploughing and other farm work was not too pressing. The farm carts were sent to the shore about two miles distant to carry back loads of seaweed which at that season was piled up in tangled masses on the beach. The seaweed was spread on the land which was later ploughed for growing turnips, but an even greater priority was to put a generous coating of seaweed on land which was later ploughed and cultivated for growing potatoes. There seemed to be elements in seaweed which ensured not only a good crop of potatoes but, more important, potatoes of excellent quality and flavour. Although neither our soil nor our climate was particularly favourable for growing potatoes, I cannot recall eating potatoes of better quality and flavour than those grown on our land which had been liberally fertilised with seaweed. It is interesting to note that 'the tangle o' the isles' is now processed and widely used as a liquid fertiliser.

One of the operations on the farm at which I was not given an opportunity to acquire skill was ploughing. The reason was simple: ploughing was an operation which was open to inspection and criticism by every passer-by, and the quality of ploughing was a matter of personal pride to the ploughman. Any ploughman worthy of the name had to satisfy himself and his fellow ploughmen, and indeed other countrymen, that his furrows were as straight as a lath and as even and uniform as the pleats on a well-tailored kilt. It was a common custom for a ploughman on a Sunday afternoon to take a long walk along country roads to inspect with critical eye the quality of work of his fellow ploughmen and, sitting on the cornkist in the stable during the following week, to express in no uncertain terms his opinion of their merits and demerits. The same pride in the quality of ploughing was shared by my elder brothers, who regularly competed in local ploughing matches, and so the only occasion on which I was allowed to handle a plough was in ploughing the endrigs, or headrigs as we called them, after the field had been ploughed.

Ploughing matches were among the few competitions which I found boring, because the technique employed at ploughing matches seemed to me to be artificial, and I failed to take them as seriously as the men who engaged in the competition. The ploughs which were generally used in ploughing matches when I was young were of a type which had really become outdated and were no longer used for everyday ploughing on the farm, but were reserved for use in ploughing matches or in practising for such competitions. While I had to admit that the 'high cut' ploughs, as we called them, could produce a beautifully shaped furrow, they demanded great effort to operate well, and the furrow which they produced did not lend itself to harrowing or cultivation as well as the furrows produced by the ploughs which were in daily use on the farms. At the time I dared not express such heretical views in my family.

My worst and most lingering memory of a ploughing match was being required, when I was a young pupil in secondary school, to transport the plough home in a farm cart after the match for a distance of about twelve miles in darkness, with one of the horses yoked to the cart and the other tied to the tail of the cart. As both horses were tired from a long day of continuous ploughing and lack of food, they walked very slowly and I did not have the heart to use the whip on them., so we progressed at less than four miles an hour. Having had no food myself since lunchtime, I stopped at the only village shop on the road, bought a packet of ginger-nut biscuits, ate the lot and suffered for my greed by feeling quite queasy before the end of the journey. At the slow pace of the weary horses I spent so much time on the road that my father feared I must have suffered an accident and sent one of my older brothers out to look for me. By the time he reached me he was so annoyed that he whipped the poor horse which was pulling the cart until it almost doubled its speed, while he berated me for my failure to speed up the two horses. For my part I just sulked and vowed to myself never again to go to a ploughing match.

One of the routine tasks in which we children took part during the Winter months was the pulling and snedding of turnips, leaving them in rows ready for loading and carting to the farm steading, where they remained in a heap until sliced in a turnip-cutter and fed to the cattle and horses as a staple part of their diet. The snedding was done with a heavy, slightly curved knife, and the process entailed wrenching the turnip from the ground, cutting off the roots with all the soil attached, then tossing the turnip aside into a row while at the same time cutting off what we called the turnip shaw. The clean cutting of the shaw while the turnip was tossed to one side demanded a fair degree of accuracy and, when the turnips were large, a fair degree of strength in a child. Because of the mild climate and relative freedom from prolonged frost in our district, the turnips were not cleared from the fields in late Autumn and stored in clamps for protection, but were left in the field over Winter and snedded only as required. Sometimes we got caught out by the frost.

I recall an occasion during the Christmas holidays when an unusually prolonged period of frosty weather occurred and then a light fall of snow. By mischance we ran short of turnips at the farm steading and my father instructed me to accompany him to the turnip field to sned a few loads of turnips. At that time I was about twelve years old and, as I recall, the turnips that year had been grown in our most upland field which was fully exposed to frost and snow. It was bitterly cold, the turnips were frozen solidly into the ground and, of course, there was no question of wearing gloves even if I had possessed gloves, which I didn't. With his big, powerful, gnarled hands my father had no difficulty wrenching the turnips from the ground and rapidly forged ahead. As for me, I had to drop the sned and use both hands with all my strength to pull the turnips from the hard-frozen ground. I had then to pick up the knife, cut off the frozen roots and, as I tossed the turnip to one side, cut off the frozen shaw. My progress was slow, my hands were soft, they gradually became so numb that they lost feeling and, with the constant wrenching at the rough stems of the turnips, the skin wore off and they started to bleed. After a time I became so miserable and so defeated at falling far behind my father that the tears began to fall. Suddenly my father stood up, walked back to me, watched my efforts for a minute or two and said quietly: 'Go hame, lad; away hame and get warmed up.' Glad to admit defeat, I turned and trotted home to the kitchen fire.

Another task which went on regularly from late Autumn until Springtime was the threshing of oats, at which the younger children were spectators rather than participants, because working at the threshing mill without due care and experience could be dangerous. Although the mill which was installed at the farm was not large it was very efficient. It was powered by an engine which was fuelled by vaporised paraffin oil and, before it could be started, the vaporising mechanism had to be heated for up to twenty minutes. The same engine was used several years later to provide the power for a suction pump, when a milking machine was installed in the byre which adjoined the barn.

In the barn were two other items of machinery: a winnowing machine which was used to clean grain, especially if it were to be sold to a seed merchant for sowing as seed, or if it were to be sent to the local mill to be ground into oatmeal for domestic use; the second item was a hay-cutter which chopped hay or straw into one-inch lengths for mixing with more concentrated food to be fed to cattle and horses. Both the winnower and the hay-cutter could be operated by hand or driven by the farm engine through a pulley and belt drive. Although strictly forbidden to use those machines, we children could not resist the temptation, when we knew father was away from home, to have a go at turning the handle. One of my fingers still bears the scar of an injury caused by careless use of the winnower. I was also guilty of removing the tip of a finger from my younger sister when she inserted a finger between the cogwheels as I was turning the handle of the hay-cutter. Both incidents left me in disgrace for quite a time.

One of the highlights of the winter for the younger children was a visit by the travelling mill which we called the big mill. The travelling mill was a massive piece of machinery which was pulled along the highway and operated on the farm by a steam engine, and usually had a working team of two men. The mill which came to our farm once a year for many years was crewed by a foreman who was hard-working and highly skilled at feeding the sheaves into the mill, and an assistant who was supposed to be responsible for keeping the steam engine oiled, fuelled with coal and topped up with water, and who was elderly, lame and lazy. He slipped out of sight and dodged work whenever possible.

The sight and sound of the big mill in operation was a source of great joy to us children, and the pleasure was heightened by the fact that for the full and efficient working of the mill at least a dozen men were required; so this was another of those occasions when neighbouring farms worked in cooperation as the mill moved from one farm to another. Preparations had to be made in the stackyard to ensure that the mill and engine were best sited for easy forking of the sheaves from the stacks to the high platform of the mill, and for the removal of the grain to a granary and the straw to a site which had been cleared for building a straw stack or'soo'as we called it locally. Likewise in the farm kitchen preparations had to be made days in advance to prepare the amount of food and drink consumed by the hungry and thirsty workers on the day when the big mill was in operation. Two men were occupied forking sheaves from the stacks to the upper platform of the mill; two men or women kneeled on the platform to unbind the sheaves and pass them to the mill foreman who fed them quickly and skilfully into the rollers and the revolving toothed drum of the mill, which began the process of threshing and winnowing the grain. At the other end of the mill, but working at ground level, two of the younger men were busy tying up the full sacks of grain, weighing not less than 200 pounds, and hoisting them on to a farm cart for transport to the granary; two men were occupied carrying the straw from the mill to the site of the straw stack, where others forked the straw up to the two men who were building the stack. My father was responsible for supervising the flow of work and also for 'keeping' the stack, ensuring that it was well and symmetrically built.

As every farmer was eager to get full value from the travelling mill, it was imperative that the mill foreman and his assistant should start work early in the morning to have the mechanism of the mill in sound working order, with every moving part oiled and greased, the engine fired to raise steam and an adequate supply of coal and water ready to hand. I can still recall a morning when the millman and my father were fussing round the mill before the men arrived from the neighbouring farms, but of the foreman's elderly helper there was neither sight nor sound. He had obviously gone to ground somewhere in the farm steading and was either in hiding or fast asleep. After shouting the old man's name at intervals but with no response, the foreman turned to my father and said: 'He's like the man's horse; he's gey ill to catch and when he's caught he's no muckle guid.'

That verdict by the millman appealed to me and has stuck in my memory because, at that time, we had on the farm a little light-grey pony known as a Welsh cob, which was yoked to a buggy that carried my father to and from town on market days and to church on Sundays. From Spring to Autumn the little pony was given free run of the pasture, which was all very well until the time came to bring her into the stable on the morning of market day or Sunday. Then the fun began, because she simply refused to be caught and, fleet of foot as she was, it sometimes took the whole family to herd her into the corner of a field; then accepting defeat she would stand with her head hanging until the halter was put on, and when yoked she would seem as docile as a well-trained pet. Despite the repeated trouble which she caused we were all very fond of her, and perhaps she would have been better behaved if the discipline had been a bit harsher. During these prolonged chases after the little pony I first realised how much I enjoyed running and that I could keep running longer than any of my brothers, although as a young child I had been the weakling of the family.

One of the minor excitements which we children and probably most of the men, though certainly not the women, anticipated with pleasure on a day of threshing by the big mill was what we called the rat hunt. It could safely be assumed that each stack held its colony of rats and mice and, as the sheaves were forked from the stack on to the platform of the mill the occasional rat would jump off the stack, but most of the rats and practically all the mice did their utmost to remain hidden until the sheaves at the bottom of the stack were being forked when the rush to escape began in earnest. As we had been taught from early childhood, and accepted without question, that rats and mice were among the farmer's natural enemies, no mercy was shown to the rats and mice trying to escape from the stack. The men armed with forks and the children with sticks joined in the hunt and did their best to ensure that as few as possible of the rodents escaped. The dogs on the farm, and even some of the cats, joined in and were often more effective than the human hunters. While the cats were usually content to seize one mouse and scamper off to play with it before killing and eating it, the dogs acquired great skill at quickly killing rat after rat. The fox terrier with whom I had played as an infant was an expert at seizing a rat by the back of the neck, giving it a lethal bite, tossing it into the air and catching it to make sure it was dead, then leaping in to seize the next rat. Inevitably some of the rats and more of the mice escaped, but in course of a day the slaughter was considerable.

One of the unusual features of our farm was a burn which ran in a stone-built conduit under the farm close and under part of the steading, and which was infested with rats. The rodent population of the farm was probably larger than normal and war was waged on them throughout the year. Along the burn-side and in the outhouses we children set traps which were inspected before and after school hours while in the farm house my father set traps for mice and poison bait for both rats and mice. In spite of our best efforts the rats and mice survived in goodly numbers, not only in the outhouses and surroundings of the farm, but also in the farm house where the sound of rats scurrying round the walls behind the wainscotting was to us a familiar sound, especially when lying in bed at night. It was a sound which held no terrors for us as it sometimes did for unwary visitors.

There was something admirable about the adaptability and cunning of the rat and about its ability to survive, as there was something admirable about its courage when cornered and its readiness to fight. I recall an incident in my late teens when I was working in a harvest field adjacent to the farm steading, forking the sheaves from the stooks on to the farm carts. Resulting from a long spell of wet weather the sheaves had stood in the field for several weeks and the bottoms were well bedded into the ground. When a cart had been loaded, if I had time in hand I pulled over some stooks to allow the sun and wind to dry the bottom of the sheaves. Under one of the stooks which I had capsized I saw a large rat which, rather to my alarm, did not scuttle away as I had expected but stood its ground and then ran straight at me. Before I could react it leaped and fixed its teeth in my old flannel trousers just below the knee. When I kicked it off with all my strength it again attacked, but this time I was ready for it and hit it with the fork. Only after killing the rat did I have an opportunity to examine the stook and found embedded in one of the sheaves a nest of grass and straw with a brood of young, naked rats, which made me realise that I had killed a mother who was intent on protecting her young.

Chapter 6
Women's Work

WHILE THE WORK OF the farm on which the male staff were chiefly engaged varied from season to season, albeit on a fairly regular pattern from year to year, what was probably the most important function of the farm in our district: the care and management of livestock and especially of the dairy herd, went on continuously, seven days a week throughout the year. In the performance of this constant, demanding work on which depended the welfare of the farm and its livestock, the tasks carried out by the women of the household were even more important than those for which the men were responsible. Apart from the workhorses for whose care and management the men were wholly responsible, the live stock on the farm included the milk cows, the young cattle from calves to two-year olds, the pigs and the hens. If some sheep were kept from time to time, my father took on the duties of shepherd. By far the most demanding of the livestock were the cows in the dairy herd, due both to their need for daily care and management and also to the heavy work imposed on the women of the household by the making of cheese and butter. As intensive farming was not generally practised in the district when I was young, the milk cows on our small farm usually numbered twenty to twenty-four. Although a milking machine was installed at a later date, the milking during my childhood was done by hand, and for the twice-daily milking my mother, a maid servant and one of my older brothers were generally responsible. Depending on whether two or three people shared in the work, the milking took between one and two hours each morning and evening.

From late Spring until Autumn the dairy cows spent day and

night in the grass parks, except when brought in for milking. In winter and early Spring they were confined to the byre every night and also during the day when the weather was inclement. Twice each day the byre was cleaned out and washed down, a process which was relatively easy when the cows were driven out to pasture, but was more onerous when the cows were kept in the byre overnight and perhaps during the day. Cleaning out the byre was one of the many tasks in which the younger members of the family were encouraged to take part. When the cows were kept in the byre they were fed twice a day on cattle cake, hay or oat straw, and sliced turnips, with plenty of water to drink. At night they were bedded with straw in their stall.

The dairy cows on our farm were Ayrshires which were not then dehorned as occurred at a later date, and an Ayrshire bull was kept to serve the cows so that calving took place in Springtime. As there was no separate calving pen the cows usually gave birth in the byre. When a cow was preparing to calve there was always a touch of anxiety lest the calving proved to be difficult or irregular. In a normal calving the two forelegs appeared first with the calf's head tucked in between them. When the head cleared the final obstruction tension eased all round, for the rest of the birth was usually quick and easy. But if only one leg appeared, or the head was twisted back, or if it gave signs of being a breach delivery then experience and skill were needed in order to ensure a live birth. If the calf proved to be lying very awkwardly, perhaps the vet might have to be called in, but such a crisis in the birth of a calf was fortunately rare. On a farm where the cows did not suckle their calves, it was important for the digestive system and future health of the calf that it be fed some of the first milk produced from the mother cow immediately after the birth. Helping in the birth of any young creature is always an uplifting experience, and I can recall few moments of greater satisfaction than when I first helped a cow in the process of calving.

When I was a child the milk produced on the farm was made into cheese, except for a small amount retained for domestic use and for making butter. From Spring to Autumn our dairy herd produced enough milk to make at least one Dunlop cheese weighing between 50 and 60 pounds when first made. Every cheese lost a few pounds in the process of maturing over a period of several months. In Winter, as the cows approached their calving season, the quantity of milk decreased until there was sufficient only to make one or two stilton-shaped cheeses of 12 to 16 pounds each.

Cheesemaking is quite a complex and lengthy process which can readily result in a spoilt or inferior product if proper standards of cleanliness and hygiene are not maintained in byre and dairy; if the required additives are not of the correct quantity, quality and standard, or if the sequence of procedures and temperature controls is not carefully observed. When I look back on it I can only conclude that the person (I could not call him an architect) who planned the position and layout of the dairy on our farm was either mentally weak or had not the slightest knowledge of the sanitary conditions desirable for the successful making of high-quality cheese. Firstly, the dairy adjoined the byre and a wide door gave direct access from the byre to the dairy; secondly, the dairy was a public thoroughfare in that everyone going between the byre and the farmhouse kitchen had to pass through the dairy; thirdly, a large water boiler fuelled by coal which raised quantities of coal-dust and ash was located within the dairy; finally a store-room as well as the butter-making room opened off the dairy which, in effect, had four doors and endless possibilities of contamination by dirt, dust and germs. Having regard to the complex nature of the process, the number of hours required every day in the year, the strict standards of hygiene to be maintained, the number of points at which the process could go wrong and the far from ideal conditions in the dairy, it seems to me a minor miracle that my mother, day after day and year after year, produced Dunlop cheeses of consistently high quality, while during the same period she brought into the world and lavished care on a family of seven children, all of whom survived to become reasonably healthy adults. In retrospect I do not find it surprising that she became exhausted and had the ill-fortune to contract pneumonia, from which she died at the early age of thirty-eight.

Cheesemaking began about 6 am when the boiler fire in the dairy was lit. As the water heated the milking of the cows proceeded and the morning's milk was added to the previous evening's milk in the cheese vat. The cheese vat was a large, rectangular container with a double skin; the inner container for holding the milk was of stainless steel, while the outer container, mounted on short legs, was made of heavier gauge metal thickly painted on the inside to prevent corrosion and heat loss, fitted with an aperture into which hot water was poured and also fitted with a tap to run off the water. When the water in the dairy boiler approached boiling point, pailfuls were poured in to fill the space between the inner and outer skins of the cheese vat, and the milk was occasionally stirred as it heated. The next step was to add a measured quantity of a 'starter' of clotted milk, which was renewed periodically from the Dairy College at Kilmarnock; then there was added a measured quantity of rennet which was derived from the stomachs of calves. The purpose of both additives was to speed up the clotting of the milk and the formation of curd, which was also aided by heating the milk to a specified temperature, at which it was maintained by running off the water which had cooled and by adding more water from the heated boiler, and also by frequent checking of a thermometer which was immersed in the milk. During the period of clotting and curd formation the milk was periodically stirred; then it was left to settle while the curd rose to the top as a thick surface coating composed of milk fat and milk solids, resting on a residual liquid known as whey. When the curd was sufficiently cooked it was cut into small cubes by the use of curd-cutters, and it was then skimmed off into a shallower vat the bottom of which was covered with wooden slats, and also with a large cheese-cloth in which the curd was tightly wrapped and left until surplus whey had been drained off. In this vat the curd slowly dried and formed into a rubbery mass. When it had reached the right consistency, the mass of curd was cut into thick strips and fed into a cutting mill which minced the curd into small pieces. After being sprinkled with salt the minced curd was filled into a 'chiset', a wooden container with strong sides bound like a barrel with steel hoops, the bottom pierced with small holes to permit drainage and a strong lid which fitted neatly inside the chiset, with two raised pieces which served as handles and also allowed pressure to be brought on the lid by a cheese-press. The well-filled chiset, the curd covered with cheese cloth and the lid in position, was placed in the cheese-press which, by means of a vertical screw, could exert the required degree of downward pressure on the lid of the chiset in order to drain, compress and solidify the curd into cheese. After being under pressure for several days, the finished cheese was removed from the chiset, rubbed all over with lard, wrapped with thin, dry cotton bandage and taken upstairs to the cheese loft, where it was stored with other cheeses on broad, wooden shelves, turned over every few days and left to mature for several months. A well-matured Dunlop cheese on our farm would weigh between forty and fifty pounds, so the regular turning of up to four dozen cheeses was quite a task.

After the curd was removed from the cheese vat the whey was run off into containers and stored, for it still contained nutrients which formed a valuable part of the mash for feeding pigs. The cheese vat and all the utensils used in making the cheese were then thoroughly sterilized with boiling water and left ready to receive the milk from the evening milking and for use on the following day. The process of cheesemaking was completed about 4pm and the evening milking began about 6pm. That gives some idea of the constant demand which a dairy farm made on those who worked in it, and especially on a housewife and mother who was also the cheese maker. The work load on my mother began every day before 6am and she was not clear of the byre and dairy before 7pm. The cradle, with a baby asleep or playing in it, often stood in a corner of the dairy where my mother could give it a little attention while the work of cheesemaking continued.

Some two or three times a year a buyer from a wholesale firm of cheese-merchants visited the farm and fixed a price for buying the matured cheese. He pierced selected cheeses with a hollow probe and drew out a sample which he smelled and tasted. having judged the quality and maturity of the cheese from the samples, he then offered a price which, as I recall, never exceeded one shilling (5p) per pound, and could be decidedly less if he decided that any of the cheese was not of top quality. As he had the experience and skill to spot a cheese which was not up to standard, he would invariably sample that particular cheese, draw attention to its inferior quality and, on that basis, offer a lower price for the whole batch. Because each buyer seemed to have a monopoly in his area and competition was non-existent, the farmer had little option but to accept the offered price. For that reason, if my father spotted a cheese which he thought might not be up to the usual high standard, he would remove it from the cheese loft and keep it for family use. Much of it could be used for cooking or as toasted cheese, but I am sorry to record that the family had on rare occasions to consume cheese with less than the best flavour in order to ensure the best price for those that were sold. On our small farm the gross income derived from the sale of cheese in a year did not exceed £600, and when the cost of rent, fertilizers, feeding stuffs, other materials and labour was deducted, the yearly profit was very small, probably less than £200; not a large return for all the time and effort required to produce the cheese, yet it was still the main source of income on the farm.

One of the ways by which farmers in our district sought to reduce the cost of feeding cattle and horses was by using the mashed grain residue, known as 'draff', from the distilleries which were still active in Campbeltown. Compared with other concentrated food for livestock the draff sold by the distilleries was relatively cheap, especially when the distilleries did not have to meet the cost of cartage. When the distilleries were working it was a common sight to see farm carts with heaped loads of draff, some still hot enough to have steam rising from it, leave the gates of a distillery and head for a farm out in the countryside. Despite the distance of our farm from Campbeltown, my father frequently sent carts for loads of draff which was mixed at the farm with other food and eaten with relish by cattle and horses. I have heard it said that draff, mixed with unrefined treacle, was a splendid feed to put animals into top condition.

The keeping of hens and pigs was a minor activity on our farm. the hens which were always on free range were generally fed and looked after by the women and children of the household who reared the chickens, prepared food for the hens, collected the eggs and cleaned out the henhouse; whereas the men of the farm merely tolerated the hens and valued them only for the eggs which were served up at the kitchen table. The farmer was content to keep a small flock of hens on free range because, at some seasons of the year, they found much of their food in and around the farm steading and were economical to maintain. To the housewife the hens were valuable for the eggs which helped to feed the family, for the surplus eggs which were sold to the grocer when his van called at the farm and for the surplus hens which from time to time were killed and plucked for the soup pot. For these reasons the hens on the farm were generally regarded as a perquisite of the housewife.

Practically every dairy farm kept some pigs, because the whey from the making of cheese and the butter-milk were valuable residues for feeding pigs but otherwise would have been waste products. My father generally kept two or three sows which were served by a boar temporarily hired for the purpose, and which produced litters of piglets to be fattened and sold either in the market or through a bargain made with a visiting dealer in livestock.

We children took a lively interest in the young pigs which were just as playful and attractive as any other group of baby creatures, whether animal or bird. When a sow produced a litter the young males had to be castrated to enable them to put on weight quickly. On one occasion when I went to look at a litter after this operation had been performed, I found that one of the piglets had suffered a serious rupture and part of its intestines trailed on the dirty floor of the pigsty. I felt so sorry for the piglet that I gathered it up in my arms, took it into the farm kitchen, washed the protruding intestine in the kitchen sink with water and disinfectant, packed the intestine as well as I could back into the abdomen, sewed it up with needle and thread and carried it back to the piggery. It survived for several days but, just as I was beginning to take pride in my surgery, it suddenly died. I mourned the loss of that little pig as if it had been a favourite pet, although I should have realised, had I been a little older, that its death was inevitable.

One of the advantages of living on a farm with livestock was the invaluable addition to the diet which we enjoyed when, as happened periodically, my father killed a pig or a sheep for family use. An incidental outcome of this practice was that we all became familiar, at an early age, with the facts of slaughter and with the sight of an animal being bled. When an animal was killed for consumption by the family, the bulk of the carcase had to last for some time and, before the advent of the domestic freezer, the methods usually employed to preserve meat were curing, drying, pickling and smoking. To ensure that the preserved meat would last as long as possible in an edible condition, it was commonly believed that the animal should be thoroughly bled at the time of slaughter. On our farm when a pig or sheep was killed for family use it was first felled to render it unconscious and then with a sharp knife a main artery was severed to allow the blood to be drained into a container. Although I can sympathise with anyone who feels squeamish or even revolted at such a crude description, for those of my generation who were brought up on a farm the process must have been taken very much for granted, as I can recall being required by my father, before I was ten years old, to hold the head of a sheep which had been placed on a shearing bench while he used a knife to bleed it into a pail. It was not a pleasant experience but it did ensure that for the rest of my life I did not flinch at the sight of blood.

When a pig had been slaughtered it was hung up by the hind legs, doused with hot water and shaved with sharp knives until all the hair and bristles had been removed, then disembowelled, cut into quarters and pickled in brine. In the meantime the organs such as liver, heart and kidneys were thoroughly washed and, after the removal of any impurities, were diced and cooked with vegetables and spices as a casserole, a dish that had a wonderful aroma and a flavour that lingered on the palate. We seldom made use of all the blood, but in some instances black puddings were made with blood mixed with minced fat and pinhead oatmeal and flavoured with spices. The major part of the carcase was boned, cured by rubbing vigorously into the meat coarse salt, saltpetre, and various peppers, then rolling the large slabs, beating with a mallet and binding tightly with ham-twine to make long rolls of bacon which were hung from the ceiling on hooks and sliced for breakfast as required. The legs were boned and cured to make hams, while the bones usually finished up in the large soup-pot. I can still recall with warmest pleasure, when coming in from the stable to the kitchen for breakfast, the smell of home-cured bacon which wafted out the door, the streaks of black pepper still visible in the rashers of bacon and the rich flavour of the mixed lean and fat, crisply fried, which set the men up for the work of the day. That was one of the memorable privileges of youth spent on a farm.

Chapter 7
Rural Services and Personalities

HAVING BEEN BROUGHT UP in a family whose religious beliefs and observance were based on the Ten Commandments and the Shorter Catechism, my father had a firm belief in the sanctity of the Sabbath: 'Remember the Sabbath day, to keep it holy. Six days shalt thou labour and do all thy work; but the seventh day is the Sabbath of the Lord thy God; in it thou shalt not do any work — —'As it was not practicable on a livestock and dairy farm to abstain from all work on Sundays, the Church bowed to the realities of the situation by sanctioning work of necessity and mercy; so on our farm the horses, pigs and hens were fed; the dairy cows were fed and milked and, as it was risky to hold the milk over for two days, the cheese was made on a Sunday. To make it clear that he observed the sanctity of Sunday, my father did not permit work in the fields on a Sunday, either by members of the family or by hired men. He also taught his children when young that they should recognise Sunday as a special day by dressing in their best clothes and being on their best behaviour, especially until after attendance at church and until after Sunday dinner. Fortunately for us, on Sunday afternoons the discipline was relaxed and I look back on these afternoons with great pleasure, for they offered several hours of leisure, free from the demands of farm work, school and church, and they offered opportunities to join with other young people in play and leisure activities, some of which were of doubtful legality. If memory serves aright, pulling the occasional salmon from the local river was as far as we went in breaking the law.

When I was young the great majority of rural families regularly attended church on Sundays, and as most families were large, this practice of regular church attendance justified the presence of two churches in the parish: the Church of Scotland or Parish Church and the United Free Church to which my family adhered and of which my father was an elder. When young we children regularly attended Sunday school, which began at 11am while the church service began at 12 noon. Sunday school ended about 11.50am and allowed us five minutes of freedom before entering church for the family service which could last till 1.30pm. As the United Free Church was located in Southend village, about 2 miles distant from our farm, attendance at church or Sunday school could entail a five-mile walk. Fortunately for us we seldom had to walk the five miles, for there was a short-cut which took us up over a hill through long grass, bracken and heather, then down the other side to the church. In wet or wintry weather we did not wear light shoes; we wore heavy boots with steel-studded soles which we called tackety boots. My father drove to church, not in a motor car but in a buggy drawn by the grey pony with the long tail. After the church service we were driven home in the buggy, and sometimes dad would hand over the reins to one of the older boys who sat up proudly as he drove the family home behind the little pony.

Among the strict rules of conduct which my father imposed on us was one at which any modern child would rebel: we were allowed to sing only hymns or psalms on a Sunday and whistling, in which I often indulged, was strictly forbidden. My clearest memory of this injunction stems from an incident which befell me after Sunday school. My teacher in Sunday school was the minister's daughter, a pretty, vivacious young lady who attracted my open admiration. On this occasion she sent me after Sunday School to the nearby manse with a message for the minister. When I knocked on the heavy front door there was no response, so I opened the door, walked into a hallway with a stair rising to the upper floor, but neither sight nor sound of the minister. As I stood there rather shyly, uncertain what to do, the minister appeared at the head of the stairs and descended, carrying some papers. Not the sight but the sound of the minister took my breath away; for he was whistling, and he was not whistling a hymn tune or a psalm tune but the tune of a then popular song. Here was the minister, a man held in awe by us children, preparing to enter the church to take a service and doing something which in my mind was a sin that would incur the wrath of God. Barely able to look at him, I gave the minister my message and scuttled out of the door, and as I went into the church I made up my mind that nobody would ever learn what I had just heard. It was my secret.

Years passed before I fully appreciated what a very good man that minister was and how fortunate we were to have the benefit of his ministry in our parish. Few people then owned a motor car, and certainly not a minister in a rural charge, who travelled all over the countryside on a bicycle, not just on the main roads but along the rough side-roads to the farms and the farm cottages. He knew all the families for many miles around, even those who seldom or never attended church. When any one was seriously ill or in trouble, the minister would be there to offer comfort and try to ensure that help was on hand. Although ever mindful that his purpose in life was to serve his community and his Master, he was full of fun and people felt better for having been in his company.

In addition to its more settled population the countryside, when I was young, sustained a number of travelling people, some of whom made a living by providing a service for rural communities, while others were eccentric or mentally disturbed people whom we called 'worthies or 'beggars', and who were generally treated with more kindness and tolerance in the countryside than they were in towns. Among those who provided services were the representatives of firms who supplied farmers with items of equipment and machinery; feeding stuffs for livestock; medical supplies and sheep dips; seeds and fertilizers and materials for ditching, draining, fencing and other essential operations on the land. Some of those men had represented the same firm, in the same part of Scotland, for the better part of a working lifetime, had become familiar figures in their area of operation and had established a friendly working relationship with farmers and their families. As they took orders from farmers for goods supplied by their firm, checked on the delivery of supplies previously ordered, received payment of accounts and, when farmers were in financial difficulties, had to exercise their judgment about extending credit, they gained over the years a valuable fund of knowledge of the general state of prosperity or decline of agriculture in their area, of the prosperity or decline of individual farms and farmers, of the personality and character of farmers and their families, and of the wisdom or otherwise of advising their firms to extend credit to farmers who had short-term or long-term financial problems. During the years of agricultural depression which prevailed in our area in the years after the first world war, there were some firms which stood almost as bankers to farmers by carrying debt and extending credit over considerable periods of difficulty.

Other regular visitors to farms were the representatives of firms who offered to buy the products of the farms: commodities like cheese, grain and potatoes; livestock including cattle, pigs, sheep, poultry and, occasionally, horses. Some of those who went round the farms seeking to purchase livestock were independent merchants or dealers, who made their living by buying and selling, and who had developed through years of experience a shrewd judgment of the quality of livestock and a wide knowledge of various markets. As a general rule those who sought to buy commodities or livestock were treated by the farmers with more caution and reserve than the representatives of the firms who were farm suppliers; for the objective of the buyers was to pay the lowest possible price and make the most favourable bargain for themselves, whereas the sellers generally sold at fixed market prices. The qualities of personality which appealed to farmers were usually possessed by the auctioneer in the local market who presided over the weekly sales of livestock and who also conducted displenishing sales or roups, as they were called, at farms which were being vacated.

In addition to the representatives of firms and individual merchants, the farms were served, as were others living in the countryside, by the regular visits of delivery vans from local shops and from shops in the nearest town. Every household in the countryside depended on being supplied by the baker, the butcher, the grocer and the fish-merchant from the vans which visited once or twice a week and which, during my childhood, were invariably drawn by horses. By virtue of these vans the rural areas were remarkably well served, as the vanmen became familiar figures to everyone, were usually very helpful and obliging, and kept to their usual rota of visits except in the most appalling weather conditions. The grocer's van, in particular, was a magnet for children because it stocked, among so many other goodies, a variety of sweets on which the children could spend their precious pennies. Some of the vanmen were also welcomed by the housewives as purveyors of local news and gossip which could enliven an otherwise unexciting day. Another visitor on whom the housewives could rely to carry the latest news and gossip was the postman, whose daily round of up to fifteen miles was done on a heavy bicycle over main roads and side roads some of which were rough and steep. Only on those rare occasions when the roads were impassable would the postman, like the delivery vans, fail to complete the scheduled round on which the rural districts relied. When I look back I am convinced that those people who lived in the countryside before the age of the motor car could depend on receiving services of the highest quality from men and women who habitually, in course of their daily round, put service before self, and frequently endured physical discomfort cheerfully and without complaint. Many people took that dependability and quality of service far too much for granted.

Among those who visited the farm from time to time I can recall two tailors: a local man who offered to measure father and sons for suits, returned later to give a fitting, then completed and delivered the suits; the other was a Jewish tailor, Mr. Finklestein, from Glasgow who offered to provide ladies' clothing, either ready-to-wear or tailored to a pattern selected by the client from a variety of patterns which he carried with him. As mothers and daughters in country districts remote from cities rarely had an opportunity to patronise dress shops, they looked forward to the visit of the travelling tailor, who did not find much difficulty in securing business from them unless the head of the family put his foot down and simply refused to provide the cash.

At a more modest level of commerce the travelling packmen, who carried their stock of goods on their back, paid a visit to the farm at irregular intervals and attempted to interest the women and girls of the household in their wares. These worthy men, who lived close to subsistence level, carried supplies of small personal and domestic items such as buttons, needles and thread, combs, hair-pins and safety-pins, pieces of lace, ribbon, tape and other materials for dressmaking; almost any kind of small, lightweight goods which met the daily needs of the family. In course of their travels these packmen soon learned which household would offer them a welcome and which would be more inclined to turn them away. As my father became known for his kindness to travelling people, a few of these packmen, who were barely able to meet the cost of even the most modest lodging, would occasionally ask permission to sleep in the barn or other outhouse of the farm. In order to make up a bed they were allowed to use hay or straw for a mattress and large sacks for covering, and supper was usually sent out to them when they had finished making their bed in the barn. The one condition on which my father insisted was that they must not light candles or matches or smoke inside the barn. If the smell of tobacco was evident after a packman had spent a night in the barn, permission to stay was never again granted.

One of my favourite packmen was old Tom Williams, whose pack was a small tin trunk with a tray for the small items like pins, needles and spools of thread. On his periodic visits to the district Tom made a habit of asking permission to sleep in our barn and, because of his cleanliness and reliability, permission was always granted. For more than thirty years Tom Williams had served his country as a soldier in the regular army, which had left its indelible marks on his character and habits. As I observed on many occasions during the 1939-45 war, the discipline of the regular army (which in many respects I detested) taught men who had served in the ranks for many years to maintain high standards of cleanliness and neatness even in the most difficult conditions, and to take for the rest of their lives a strong pride in their bearing and personal appearance. The discipline and training of the regular soldier were always apparent in old Tom's manner and dress, in his habit of washing the dishes and cutlery after he had eaten his supper and in the care with which he made his bed in the barn. Before making his bed he selected with care some large sacks and one small sack, which he carried to the daylight at the barn door and there removed every speck of chaff, grain or dirt; he then formed a neat mattress of hay or straw, covered it with one or more large sacks, filled the small sack with hay as a pillow and used the remaining large sacks as blankets. When his bed had been carefully made he would come to the barn door to smoke his clay pipe, and there he charmed us children with tales of his life as a soldier in Egypt, the Sudan, the North-West Frontier and Afghanistan. When, during the nineteen eighties, a long and futile war was fought in Afghanistan, I could recall from the tales of old Tom Williams the vivid description which he gave of a forced march which the British troops had made from Kabul to Kandahar under the leadership of General Roberts, who later became Lord Roberts. Although these romantic-sounding names remained in my memory, I had no idea where in the world Kabul and Kandahar were situated, but old Tom left us in no doubt that he had fought in all kinds of lands from burning deserts to high and rugged mountains, and always against wily and dangerous enemies who repeatedly laid an ambush for British soldiers.

Another group of periodic visitors were the travelling folk, at that time more commonly known as tinkers, of whom there were two main groups in the district: the Townsleys and the Williamsons, who travelled the roads from late Springtime till the onset of Winter, when they preferred to remain in a more settled encampment. During the past generation efforts have been made by local authorities and others, with limited success, to have travelling folk housed in settled communities. As an alternative, local authorities with the encouragement of central government have endeavoured to reserve and equip permanent sites with hygienic facilities for the caravans and tents of travelling folks. Among the reasons for such endeavours has been the growing reluctance of those who own or occupy land to grant travelling folk sites and facilities for encampment. It seems to me that tinkers are now widely regarded as having no real function in the community and therefore no acceptable place in the community.

When I was young the tinkers had sites throughout the district on which they could erect their tents with confidence, provided that they did not stay too long in one place, and so long as their conduct did not outrage the local landowner or tenant farmer. Although most of the tinker families, especially the women and children, went round the farms begging for food and clothing, there still remained in every community a large measure of acceptance of the tinkers, because they still performed a useful function in the rural economy. Their two main skills were as tinsmiths and basket-weavers, whereby they made useful articles for sale or barter in course of their travels round the district. Before the era of milk bottles and plastic containers, every household used as receptacles tin cans, metal pails and pitchers, and that applied especially on livestock and dairy farms which were universal in our district. In addition to the making of these items, the men of the tinker families would repair and solder any utensils which leaked or had lost a handle. Equally useful on the farms were the large oval baskets which the tinkers wove from willow canes on hazel frames, and which were commonly used for harvesting potatoes behind the mechanical potato digger, and also for carrying foodstuffs to cattle, horses and sheep. In one sense the tinkers who made and repaired metal containers and wove baskets for use on farms could be regarded as craftsmen who were among the last of their kind to be overtaken by the first industrial revolution. In other words they competed with the factory-made product for longer than the great majority of handicraft workers, but during my lifetime the mass-produced factory product defeated them and made their craft-skill obsolete. As a consequence the tinkers lost their main function in the rural community.

The second function of the tinkers was to provide casual, short-term help on farms during periods when extra hands were welcomed: help with singling turnips, working behind the reaper at the grain harvest and working behind the potato digger at the potato harvest. When the acreage of turnips grown on farms decreased following the introduction of silage; when the binder replaced the reaper in the harvest field and when potatoes were grown mainly for domestic use, the demand for casual labour also decreased and the tinkers became less welcome on the farms. For more than two centuries economic progress, based on mechanical and technological innovation, has resulted in the loss of function and the redundancy of many workers who offered the community a service based on craft skill; such fate overtook the tinkers in my generation.

Among the travelling families who regularly visited our district the largest, the most vigorous and the most rumbustious were the Townsleys. When I was a child the head of the family was old Jock Townsley, a strong character who was respected in the travelling community but who died before I was of age to take an interest in the travelling folk. While one would have expected a brother or son to assume the leadership of the clan, the mantle of real authority appeared to fall on big Nancy, who may have been Jock Townsley's wife. I recall her as a tall woman of strong build and strong features, with a strong voice, a fondness for strong tobacco smoked in a clay pipe and, reputedly, a fondness for a dram of good, strong whisky. She and her family had travelled round the district for so many years that she knew every family in the countryside, and she also knew the details of every local scandal and the skeletons kept in family cupboards throughout the district.

My father once told me of an incident relating to Nancy which he had witnessed when in town on a market day. As Nancy and some of her family were passing through the town they occasionally begged a little money for a drink from farmers whom they knew well. On this occasion when a request for the price of a dram was abruptly refused and the farmer turned to walk away, Nancy followed him down the street and shouted at the top of her powerful voice all the scandalous titbits which she had picked up about that farmer's family in course of her travels. My father expressed the opinion that, by the time Nancy had finished her recital, the farmer concerned had ample cause to regret his refusal of the price of a dram. One of the most pleasing features of the travelling folk was their love of singing and storytelling and the talent which some of the men had for playing the bagpipes. Among the travelling folk who had served as soldiers in the war of 1914-18, a few had obviously been given the opportunity to develop their knowledge and skill as pipers, a skill which they later used to earn money as buskers.

Their rather precarious mode of life, their frequent movement from one camp site to another, their rudimentary tents, their exposure to inclement weather, their uncertain earnings, the variable standard of their food and clothing and their difficulty in securing prompt medical attention probably made the travelling folk peculiarly subject to the law of survival of the fittest. One of the vivid memories of my youth bears testimony to the physical toughness and powers of endurance of those who did survive the rigours of the travellers' life to reach an advanced age. On a warm summer evening, after a day of work in the hayfield, I was standing at the barn door with the men of the farm when George Townsley, one of the elders of the clan, came hurrying towards us along the road and paused to inquire if we had seen his family on the road. He was obviously weary, sweat dripped from his face, his shirt clung damply to his body and he gladly accepted a drink from the pitcher which I had carried in from the hayfield. About a week previously, after some drink taken, George had collided with a motor car in Campbeltown, which left him with severe bruising and a few broken ribs. He was taken to the local hospital where he was washed, had his broken ribs set, his body swathed with yards of sticking plaster and was confined to bed. Before his ribs were healed he managed to get dressed and, evading the nursing staff, he walked out of the hospital in the hope of joining his family.

Having learnt that they had set up camp in Southend, he walked twelve miles to their usual camp site, only to find that they had left on the same day and had taken the circular road round the parish on their way back to Campbeltown. Old George had followed on, hoping to overtake them, and by the time he had arrived at our farm he had walked fourteen miles in his semi-invalid condition in one of the warmest days of the summer. When we were able to tell him that his family had passed along the road earlier that afternoon, he refused our offer to let him sleep in the barn overnight and, after eating a sandwich of bread and jam while displaying the swathes of bandage round his ribs, he insisted on resuming his walk in the hope of overtaking his family before the onset of darkness. For a man of his age and physical infirmity it was a remarkable display of obstinacy and endurance which I could not but admire and have never forgotten.

Among the most hopeless of the travelling folk were the real beggars who gave no service, but depended wholly on begging from door to door for their sustenance, and on finding somewhere to sleep in an outhouse or in a cave or in the shelter of a haystack. One such was the man whose name was unknown to us but whom, when we were children, we called 'The Jostler'. Under current welfare provisions the Jostler would have been treated as a patient suffering from mental illness, but in our rural community he was regarded as a 'worthy' and, as he did no harm to anyone except himself, he was left to roam the countryside at will, almost wholly dependent for clothing, food and shelter on the goodwill of householders. When I knew him he was probably middle-aged but, in his unkempt, unshaven and ragged condition he appeared to us children as an ancient scarecrow. His outstanding quality was his extreme timidity and fear of anything unfamiliar, which left him with an irresistible feeling of being jammed or jostled by groups of people, herds of cattle, flocks of sheep, or by the sudden appearance of a motor car or truck, or even by meeting a group of children who jeered and called him names. On feeling the urge to escape from anything which jammed or jostled him, he would shout aloud and would dash off the road, over the boundary fence or through the hedge into the nearest fields. If in course of his rush to escape his clothing caught in a thorn hedge or on barbed wire, he made no attempt to undo the snag but forcibly wrenched until the article of clothing was torn or part of it left hanging where it was snagged. As a result of these repeated escapades he was invariably dressed in rags and tatters and, as he did not always remove the remains of an old, torn coat when he put on a better coat which some kindly housewife had given to him, he did often merit the description of scarecrow or tattie-bogle. When I look back I am ashamed of the way in which we children treated the Jostler, but there is no group more callous than schoolboys and, at the time, it appealed to us as good fun, especially since the poor, timid man posed no threat to us.

During my childhood one of the tradesmen who provided a most essential service to the farming community was the blacksmith. In the days before the motor car, the tractor and the truck, the farmers depended entirely on horses as the motive power both for farming operations and for road transport and, in order to work efficiently, horses required to have their shoes replaced at regular intervals. Because of the large number of heavy workhorses and ponies on the farms, and because of the constant work required to repair and maintain a great variety of farm tools and equipment, the blacksmiths in two separate smithies, or 'smiddies' as we called them, were kept fully occupied in the parish. One of these smiddies was located on a small croft adjoining our farm and, of course, it was a permanent magnet for us children who spent happy hours watching the blacksmith at work, heating the iron bars in the forge, the fire kept hot by the forced draught from the bellows; then hammering the red-hot iron on the anvil into a horse shoe, or a tine for a harrow, or a welding piece to repair the coulter of a plough, while the fiery sparks flew from the metal and the hammer beat out a rhythmical, bell-like clangour on the anvil. When a set of four horse shoes, had been fashioned, it was fascinating to watch the blacksmith, with bare arms and leather apron tied round his ample waist, approach the next horse to be shod with a rasp or curved knife in his hand, pat the horse on the neck, speak to it quietly, then lift a foreleg by the fetlock, tuck it between his knees and file the hoof to a balanced shape with the rasp or dress it with the knife. It was equally interesting to watch the smith fit to the hoof the metal shoe which had been gently heated in the forge and smell the acrid smoke from the burning hoof as the shoe was clamped to it, while the smith hammered in the shoenails with the skill that brought through the hoof the tip of each nail, which was then bent over to prevent the shoe from being cast before it was fully worn down. When the forefeet had been shod the smith moved to the hind legs with confidence that the horse was now accustomed to his movements and much less inclined to kick.

Since there was no simple way, before telephones were installed, to make prior appointments, a queue of men leading horses to be shod or driving carts containing farm implements to be repaired quite often formed at the smiddy, which became known throughout the farming community as a centre for the exchange of local news and gossip. The smiddy was a nice, cosy, fuggy place, especially in cold and wintry weather, for men to gather for a smoke and chat while the horses were tethered outside awaiting their turn to be shod. Some of the younger men were keen to help the blacksmith by wielding a heavy hammer at the anvil, or by assisting with one of the more difficult and exacting jobs such as fitting a new metal rim to the wheel of a farm cart. In order to have the circular rim uniformly heated, the smith had to build a specially large fire on the hearth and have help in moving the heavy rim on the forge while the bellows was kept active to maintain the heat. When the rim had been heated to the smith's satisfaction, he required the help of at least one other man with heavy tongs to lift the rim and fit it over the wooden wheel, which had been laid flat on a circular, concrete base with a large hole in the centre to take the nave of the wheel. When the iron rim was cooled it contracted just sufficiently to clamp itself snugly round the wheel, which would give many years of wear before another new rim was required. From watching the blacksmith renew the rim of a cartwheel children could learn a useful practical lesson about the physical properties of metal.

When I was a child our local blacksmith died while still a young man, and the smiddy was taken over by Walter Campbell, who had been born and brought up in the Highlands but had worked for several years as a blacksmith in Glasgow. The children in our family learned with satisfaction that the new blacksmith had a family of six sons and a daughter, and although the older members of the family were grown men, the two youngest boys were still of age to attend our local school and share in our leisure ploys. To our pleasure and surprise we soon found that, despite having been brought up in a city, they knew more than we did about opportunities for keeping the family kitchen supplied with game from the land and fish from the sea and the river.

Although he was probably still in his fifties Walter Campbell, because of his shock of strong, grizzled hair, soon became known to everyone as Old Wattie, while one of the older sons was called Young Wattie. Old Wattie was a great talker with a natural gift for telling stories of which he seemed to have an endless fund, especially stories of the supernatural: of ghosts and witches and kelpies and bockans, and people with second sight, and wee folks who lived underground among the rocks and hills to appear only in darkness to steal young lambs and young babies from their cots. He was full of superstition and seemed to believe the many tales which he told with such flair and fluency, as apparently did his family who had heard them repeatedly.

I was of an age to find Old Wattie's stories quite absorbing and I must admit that an evening spent listening to his tales was enough to set the nerves on edge and make any child afraid of the darkness. I recall just such a night when I was out with one of the Campbell boys seeking to catch rabbits on our farm, and returned with him to the smiddy for supper. After listening to some of Old Wattie's tales of the West Highlands I set out for home in a quiet, pitch-black night, with no moon shining and no stars visible. One of the Campbell sons kindly gave me an old bicycle lamp, at that time fuelled by acetylene, which gave me just enough light to find my way along the road. As I walked cautiously along I suddenly heard a rustle behind the roadside hedge, followed by a hard coughing sound, 'uck! uck!' and when I turned the lamp in that direction two amber eyes gleamed in the darkness. I ran for my life and did not stop until I fell headlong into the roadside ditch. Only then did I begin to think clearly enough to realise with shame that I had been scared by nothing worse than an old sheep.

My close friend among the Campbell family was Donnie, who was somewhat older than I and who had already become, under the tutelage of his older brothers, a very accomplished poacher. Donnie it was who taught me the art of catching trout with a running loop of wire from a rabbit snare, firmly bound on the end of a long hazel rod, a device which we called a 'snigger'. For snigging trout a loop made from a single strand of copper wire was strong enough, but if one wished to graduate to snigging a salmon, then a strong rabbit snare tied firmly on the end of the rod was the standard equipment. The art of snigging as taught me by the Campbell brothers was to keep still, hidden as much as possible from the intended prey, and almost always work the snigger slowly and carefully over the tail, not over the head of the fish. With these sniggers we caught brown trout, sea trout and, much more rarely, salmon in the deep, clear pools of the local river. The snigging or guddling of a few trout was generally regarded by the river proprietors as a boyish prank to which little objection was taken, but the snigging of a salmon was a dangerous and exciting ploy, for if caught in the act by a gamekeeper, the young poacher could expect no mercy. For that reason, when I accompanied my friend Donnie on an expedition to the river, I usually persuaded him to restrict his skill to the snigging of trout.

The Campbell family kept a dog which was the best rabbit catcher of any dog that I have known; better than a greyhound, although I would back the greyhound in pursuit of a hare. Many an evening Donnie and I spent roaming over the hill land of our farm with the dog in pursuit of rabbits for the pot. The dog had been trained, when he caught a rabbit, not to kill it but to bring it alive to Donnie, just like a trained retriever. One night when we were walking over the rough ground of the hill, the dog was working along the side of a gully which was thickly covered with brambles, bracken and gorse. Suddenly out of the gully he brought a rabbit to Donnie who bent down and took it from the dog's mouth, stared almost unbelievingly at the rabbit, then shouted: 'My God, it's a witch, it's a witch!' and hurled the rabbit from him back into the gully. I immediately plunged into the gully after the rabbit and spent a long time, along with the dog, trying to find it, but it was obviously still fully alive and had escaped into a burrow among the brambles and gorse.

Over the years I have greatly regretted the loss of that rabbit, for it was a marvel of nature and would have graced any wildlife museum. Although I was given only a few seconds to see the rabbit, what I saw was perfectly clear and never to be forgotten. The two front teeth in the upper jaw had grown to, I would estimate, upwards of three inches in length; they were quite symmetrical and were curved up over the rabbit's head like miniature tusks of a mammoth. It was so unusual and unexpected that it proved too much for my superstitious friend Donnie.

I went home and told my family of our experience but I am not sure that anyone fully believed me. With the passing of the years I sometimes began to wonder if I had actually seen what I thought I saw, for no rabbit catcher or other countryman whom I met could report having seen or heard of such a curiosity. A few years ago, on a visit to Blair castle with my family, I walked through a room which had recently been opened to the public and which had on display many specimens of animals, birds, fish and trophies of the hunt. There among the stuffed animals was a rabbit with the kind of long, curling tusks which I have just described, although it is not such a perfect specimen as the one which my friend's dog caught and which I briefly saw these many years ago. It gave me a thrill of pleasure and relief to see that rabbit at Blair Castle, as it confirmed for the first and only time in more than sixty years that such a phenomenon could actually occur and that my boyish eyes had not deceived me. One aspect which still puzzles me is how a rabbit with such tusks succeeded in feeding itself and in looking as healthy as that which I saw.

A few years after seeing the rabbit with the overgrown teeth, I had the experience of finding on the farm another example of the unusual works of nature, an experience which has not been shared by any nature lover of my acquaintance. While still in my early teens I was walking over the fields with a terrier dog and a twelve-bore shot gun, when the dog suddenly paused and pointed at something along the side of a boundary ditch. I called the dog off and walked on fully expecting a rabbit to run or a bird to rise. Then I caught sight of a partridge, half concealed in the grass and obviously unable to fly. When I carefully picked it up I observed that it was seriously injured; a patch of skin and feathers somewhat smaller than the palm of my hand had been torn off one side, partially covered by its wing, perhaps through collision with an overhead telephone line. The marvel was that this extensive wound had been covered with the utmost neatness and care by a dressing of tiny leaves, overlapping like scales on a fish or like tiles on the roof of a toy house. While I was holding it very tenderly the bird wriggled out of my hand and crept back into the cover of the ditch where I did not have the heart further to disturb it. Only after I had walked on for some distance did it strike me, to my lifelong regret, that I failed to recognise from what type of lichen or other plant the tiny leaves had come. It would have been interesting to ascertain whether the tiny leaves had medicinal qualities. I never again saw such a phenomenon, nor have I met anyone who did.

Two persons of authority, or representatives of authority,

whom we children held in respect were the local policeman and the gamekeeper: the policeman as the agent of the law and the gamekeeper as the agent of the landowner. Well we knew that we had no cause to fear either, so long as we refrained from serious misbehaviour, but my memory leaves the impression that both of these figures of authority served as checks on the conscience of many of us as we grew from childhood into youth. The only breach of the law which I can recall in the company of my school chums was the competitive throwing of small stones at what we called 'the telegraph cups', which were the ceramic insulators on the telephone wires high up on the telephone poles which at that time fringed the sides of all main roads. The ability to throw stones accurately was one of the minor ambitions shared by almost all country boys, and if anyone succeeded in hitting an insulator, which in my experience rarely happened, he could boast of it for weeks. Most of the damage to insulators was actually caused by loutish youths and young men who persisted in competitive stone throwing long after they had left school.

Before the advent of the motor car the country police officer and the gamekeeper, like others who had to travel many miles on country roads, generally used a sturdy bicycle to cover their territory. Our local gamekeeper was employed by the principal landowner, the Duke of Argyll, to encourage the breeding and maintenance of grouse, partridges, pheasants and other game birds which, in terms of their lease, were not the property of the tenant farmer but remained the property of the landowner. It was the duty of the gamekeeper to protect all game birds from slaughter except by permission of the landowner; likewise it was his duty to ensure that only those persons with a permit were allowed to fish for or otherwise catch salmon and sea trout in the local rivers. The gamekeeper was well aware that, in carrying out his duties he was up against a belief held by most people brought up in the rural areas of Scotland that, though it was technically illegal it was not morally indefensible to catch a pheasant or a salmon occasionally for a family meal. He was also aware that some people with whom he was on familiar and friendly terms in course of his work would happily shoot a game bird or catch a salmon when the gamekeeper was not in the vicinity. Fortunately for the work of the gamekeeper, most of the people who would have no qualms about shooting a game bird or catching a fish for their family would object as strongly as he to large-scale poaching of game or salmon. In a district where livestock formed an important element of farming, the systematic theft of animals was regarded as a serious crime, and large-scale poaching was looked on as theft.

One of the accepted features of the rural scene was the arrival each year of the shooting tenants to whom the factor of the Argyll Estates had let the shooting rights over an area which comprised a group of farms, and which usually included moorland and arable land to provide a variety of sport. The shooting tenants were generally wealthy men who invited a party or parties of guests, many from England or farther afield, to join them in the sport of shooting grouse on the moors and, later in the season, shooting pheasants, partridges, woodcock and other game on the lower ground. The annual visits of the shooting tenants and guests were warmly welcomed by hoteliers, shopkeepers and others who benefited from their patronage, and were also welcomed by casual labourers and young people who served as beaters to drive the game on to the guns. The shooting season was one of the busiest periods of the year for the gamekeeper who had responsibility for siting, building and maintaining the shooting butts on the moors, for helping to organise the shoots and, for recruiting and supervising the men and youths who were employed as beaters. Some of the shooting tenants who rented the same moors year after year became well-known and respected figures in the local community.

One representative of authority, the exciseman, who in previous generations had frequent cause to visit the rural districts had become practically unknown by the time I was born, except in the distilleries and bonded warehouses of Campbeltown. The three activities in our district which had, in the nineteenth and earlier centuries, attracted the attention of the excise officers were organised smuggling, illegal distilling of whisky and the plundering of ships which were wrecked on the coasts of Kintyre. Before the arrival of motor vehicles Kintyre, like the islands of Scotland, had traditionally been dependent on transport by sea for its trade and commerce with the mainland of Scotland, and also for its commercial links with Ireland, which in previous centuries had been much closer and more extensive than in recent times. By virtue of its situation and the number of places round the coast at which boats habitually called, it was relatively easy to ship small cargoes, legal or illegal, into and out of Kintyre without attracting undue attention. I was told by an aged relative (but have no further evidence) that forebears of my family had been for a time tenants on the island of Sanda, about three miles off Southend, and according to gossip made a better living from smuggling than they did from herding sheep.

Smuggling frequently involved the products of illegal distilling. When I was young many were the tales of the small pot stills which had been located in the remote glens and round the rocky shores of Kintyre, and many the stories of the families who made part of their living from illegal distilling of whisky, and of the ingenious methods which they employed to conceal their activities and deceive the excise officers, whose constant endeavour was to discover the stills and suppress the illegal trade. As Kintyre had larger areas of fertile ground than most parts of the West Highlands, supplies of grain were produced in such quantity that the amounts diverted for illegal distilling could not easily be detected. While in many instances the small volume of whisky distilled was consumed by the family or shared among neighbours, there was a sufficient surplus from the stills concealed in remote parts of the countryside to justify a measure of organised smuggling of liquor from Kintyre to other areas of Scotland and this was usually done by boat. The efforts of the excise officers to trap the smugglers in the act of transporting supplies of whisky sometimes resulted in violence and bloodshed, when the smugglers either escaped or more often finished up in court. When I was young I heard many stories of ships which had been wrecked either on the reefs near the Island of Sanda or on the shores of Southend, especially when land and sea were wreathed in thick mist which quite often blanketed the whole peninsula from the Mull of Kintyre to Campbeltown. While everyone mourned the death of seamen there were, according to these stories, people living close by the sea who welcomed cargo from a wrecked ship as an opportunity to add some excitement and a few luxuries to what was otherwise a rather drab, impoverished life. Although most of the stories referred to ships which had been wrecked before I was born, I can recall from my childhood my elder brothers returning from the seashore, from which they had been carting seaweed, with barrels of a thick grease which they claimed was palm-oil and which must have been washed ashore from ships sunk at sea during the 1914-

The author's mother and father, c. 1904.

The author's father with seven children, c. 1922.

The location of Low Cattadale; farm buildings in centre.

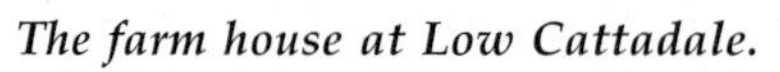

The farm house at Low Cattadale.

Part of the stackyard at Low Cattadale.

A break for tea in the hayfield.

A farm cart with flat frames for carting hay or sheaves.

A reaper cutting a crop of oats.

A three horse binder.

The travelling mill in operation.

The blacksmith shoeing a horse in the smiddie.
The stage coach which made a return journey between Campbeltown and Tarbert daily until 1914.

The author's children feeding a pet lamb from a bottle.

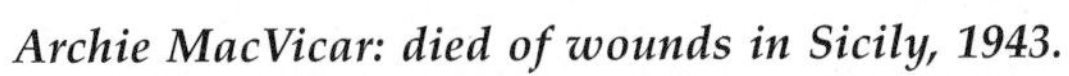

Archie MacVicar: died of wounds in Sicily, 1943.

A German tank, equipped with 88mm high velocity gun.

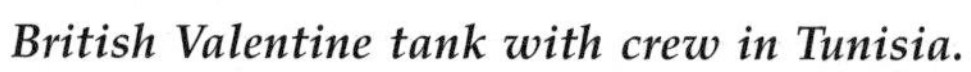

British Valentine tank with crew in Tunisia.

18 war. The grease was used mainly for lubricating the axles of farm carts and other heavy implements and, as I recall, it met the needs of the farm for many years.

One of the more amusing stories which were told in my youth referred to the wreck of a ship with the French name of Charlemagne, which ran aground on a lonely part of the Southend shore, and from which the crew were rescued with the help of local people. The ship was apparently accessible at low tide and, as the wreck occurred before the advent of motor transport and the nearest excise officers were stationed in Campbeltown, many of the local people had ample opportunity to explore the wreck before the excisemen could arrive on the scene. Among the ship's cargo was a large quantity of whisky most of which was spirited ashore and hidden long before the arrival of the excise officers. According to the tale which was related to me, the removal of the cargo was followed by a drinking spree which lasted so long that some of the people concerned could not afterwards recall where all the bottles had been concealed, with the result that occasional bottles were discovered years later in unexpected hiding places. Because the name 'Charlemagne' was meaningless to many of the local inhabitants, the whole episode became generally known and remembered as the wreck of the 'Charlie Man'.

Many years later a story which related to the wreck of the Charlemagne was told by a shooting tenant who was leading a shooting party over one of the moors near that part of the coast on which the wreck had occurred. While the party was traversing the moorland, it became enveloped in one of the impenetrable mists which can suddenly blow in from the sea around Southend. In the swirling fog they became utterly lost and were quite alarmed until by chance they met an elderly shepherd with his dog. When the shooting tenant asked his advice about how to find his way off the hill the shepherd referred him to the foghorn on the island of Sanda, which sounded its deep note at regular intervals. 'Dae ye hear that blasted foghorn', said he, 'weel, keep that sound on yer left lug and walk on till ye come tae a wee burn. Follow the burn doon the brae till ye reach the main road and ye'll be a'right'. Then as he turned away the old shepherd said half to himself: 'And dang the noisy thing; there hasna been a good wreck on this shore since the Charlie Man ran aground.'

Chapter 8
The Big School

WHILE I WAS STILL IN attendance at our local school a major change took place in our family life, when my father resolved to remarry and we children, much to our surprise, found that we had gained a stepmother. A few years earlier our housekeeper, Phemie, in common with many other people from Scotland, seized an opportunity to emigrate to Canada. Why she so decided I never discovered, but it may have been an urge to improve her lot or it may have resulted from some disagreement with my father who, as I have already remarked, had a quick and unpredictable temper. If my father was in some manner responsible for her decision to emigrate he must soon have had cause to regret it, for he failed to find anyone who was prepared to accept the domestic responsibilities and the burden of work with the livestock and in the dairy which Phemie had borne since the death of my mother. He must finally have written to her, without the knowledge of any of the family, pleading with her to return and offering her marriage. For reasons known only to herself Phemie did return to the farm and became our stepmother. In due course she gave birth to three children: William, born in 1926; Alexander (Sandy), born in 1930 and Phemie, born in 1937. Our family of seven thus grew to ten children which, even in those days, was a very large family. About the time of my father's second marriage I became eligible for transfer to secondary school, which took me away from home except at weekends and major holidays, so this important change in our family life may have had less effect on me than on other members of the family.

At the unusually advanced age of thirteen I sat the qualifying examination for transfer to secondary school and in August, 1924 I began academic course at Campbeltown Grammar School. Although my three elder brothers had passed the qualifying examination, none of them was allowed to transfer to secondary school because my father felt that he required their help on the farm. When our parish minister, who was a member of the Education Authority, told my father that the marks which I had scored in the qualifying examination were among the highest in the county of Argyll, and that the Authority would award me a bursary he decided that I could be spared from the work of the farm, to become what was locally called 'a scholar'. As a bus service for those pupils from Southend who attended Campbeltown Grammar School was run only on Monday mornings and Friday afternoons, it was necessary for the children to stay in lodgings during the week. I recall that my first landlady was a widow named Mrs. McSporran, a good Highland name borne by several families in Kintyre but which I later discovered, to my surprise, was regarded by many as a name invented by a Scots comedian for the music hall stage. I later lodged with a married lady, Mrs. McLean, who looked after four of us pupils with great kindness.

On Monday mornings my father roused me before six o'clock and, after a hurried breakfast, I stuffed my belongings for the week into my satchel and walked for about a mile, in all weathers to the road junction where I boarded the bus shortly after seven o'clock. As the bus in those days did not travel at more than thirty miles per hour, and had frequent stops to pick up passengers. I reached my lodgings in Campbeltown at about eight o'clock, sorted out my belongings to leave only textbooks in my satchel and set off for school to meet my classmates. For a shy child from a lonely farm and a small rural school, transfer to secondary school and life in lodgings imposed some strain and tension which wore off only in time, but my transition was aided by the fact that I was older and rather more mature than most of my fellows. My greater maturity also helped me to cope more readily with the new subjects introduced at secondary school and thus eased my adaptation to the new life.

Secondary education at that time as exemplified by the academic courses at Campbeltown Grammar School offered a rather dreary, uninspired, uninspiring and spartan diet, not by any means lacking in nourishment but almost completely devoid of enrichment, imagination and interest and anything that might tempt the appetite or leave a pleasant aftertaste on the palate. One of the few exceptions to that stricture was English as taught by the Head of Department, a man of scholarship, imagination and sensitivity who obviously cherished his subject and under whom I had the privilege of studying during the later years of my secondary course. During my six years at the school there were no extracurricular activities, no organised sport, no planned visits or excursions, no school concert or school play, no school library (apart from some books in the classroom of the Principal Teacher of English) the very minimum of equipment and no study materials other than essential textbooks. In course of normal classroom work, except for the sixth year, opportunities for discussion or any active contribution by the pupils were almost completely lacking; group activity and cooperation among pupils were positively and sometimes brutally discouraged. Ability to memorise was prized and rewarded far above the ability to think constructively or to engage in creative, cultural or purposeful activity. I can recall only one teacher, an unmarried man of middle age, who encouraged boys to take an interest in sport after school hours, and only because he was obsessively keen on cricket.

The dull and uninspired curriculum of the school was fortunately leavened by the engaging characteristics and personalities of some of our teachers. Among them was old Dougie, a man of dry humour and unruffled temperament, who contrived to teach the early stages of Algebra and Geometry while spending most of his time lounging in his armchair in front of the class. Even the diagrams on the blackboard, which was used to a minimum, were sometimes drawn to his instructions by one of the brighter pupils. His ability to maintain discipline seemed to be effortless, as he could very quickly size up the pupils in a class and spot potential troublemakers who were shrivelled by his sharp tongue.

In marked contrast was our teacher of elementary science, a man who had served as an officer in the 1914-18 war and was a highly respected member of the local community. Despite his record as a soldier and his standing among the citizens of the town; despite his apparent lack of any eccentricity in appearance, demeanour or dress; and despite his ability and willingness to wield the tawse with power and precision, he failed to imbue pupils with either fear or respect and he signally failed to maintain discipline in the laboratory. The disorder which ensued, especially among the boys in his classes, reflected badly on the status of Science which was generally held in low esteem throughout the school.

In later life when I had, among many other duties, the normally pleasant responsibility of interviewing and recruiting young teachers, I found that one of the most difficult aspects of the task was to assess their ability to maintain order and discipline in a classroom. Whether a young teacher found it easy or difficult to maintain discipline depended largely on qualities of personality which were not always obvious to another adult outwith the classroom situation, but seemed to become obvious almost immediately to pupils in a classroom. I found it fascinating to watch how a young slip of a girl could walk into a classroom and immediately have senior boys and girls under what seemed effortless control, though physically they were much more powerful than the teacher, while occasionally a strong, well-built and personable man would fail miserably to gain the respect of pupils. Admittedly there are techniques and methods which can be taught to help inexperienced teachers improve their class discipline, and fortunately self-confidence often improves with teaching experience, but for some people there is no alternative but to recognise and accept that teaching is the wrong profession.

The ability to maintain discipline presented no problem to Kate and Lizzie two sisters of mature years who had given long service in the school and who were capable of teaching a variety of subjects to pupils in the early years of their secondary course. Kate, in particular, was a lady of formidable personality and forthright manner who taught us Latin in the first year of our course. With hindsight I am inclined to think that Kate's knowledge of Latin was limited, but it was certainly adequate for teaching the elements of grammar to pupils in their first year, and it would be difficult to conceive of a more thorough grounding in the first stages of Latin grammar than we received from Kate. However limited her objectives and however narrow the field which she covered, the grammar which Kate taught was retained for life.

I recall that, in our first term examination, a goodly number of pupils had no errors and could boast a perfect score. In a test at the end of the second term a few pupils still had no errors and were warmly commended by Kate, who then fixed a cold eye on one of my pals who had achieved a perfect score in the first term test. 'And now you, Galbraith', she rasped, 'I knew you would make a mess of it; I just knew you would fail; you scored only 84%!' It was quite obvious that the only standard that would secure Kate's approval was perfection.

As a teacher of long standing who had spent her life in the town, Kate had taught the parents of several pupils who were in my class at school and had no hesitation in taking advantage of her experience to visit the sins of the parents on the children. On one occasion a rather pretty, pert girl incurred Kate's wrath by making a somewhat cheeky remark. After withering the poor girl with a cold blast of sarcasm Kate finished by saying: 'And you, miss, you have the cheek to sit there with your face of brass, just as your mother sat before you!'

The member of staff who encouraged the boys to play cricket was the Principal Teacher of Mathematics, known to all the pupils as Big George, not so much on account of his stature as in recognition of his massive frame and powerful shoulders, which made it easy to envisage him standing solidly at the crease and hitting balls over the boundary with consummate ease. The boys, in particular, could all the more readily accept his skill with the bat because of their experience of the power and accuracy with which he wielded the tawse in class, which he did infrequently but with great ceremony and to awesome effect. When a boy was about to be punished, George would ask the class to turn their eyes away, but of course we looked, as I have no doubt that he knew we would, sorry for the victim while inwardly praying that we should never incur his wrath. In the Mathematics classroom exemplary discipline prevailed. I cannot ever recall him giving physical punishment to a girl.

Big George was a bachelor who had permanent accommodation in a local hotel and gave the impression of being a loner to whom the only activities of importance in the school were Mathematics and cricket. When he gave the pupils homework, as he frequently did, he made it clear that the work in Mathematics took precedence over all other homework and the pupils responded accordingly. As a teacher of Mathematics he was systematic and thorough and, because of the application and effort which he demanded from his pupils he had a well-earned reputation in the school for his consistent success in getting pupils through examinations in higher Mathematics. With hindsight I feel that his greatest weakness was a failure to illustrate and illumine the principles of his subject, especially to those pupils who were not mathematically inclined, by giving examples of the application of Mathematics to the solution of problems in everyday life. I cannot recall, for instance, any reference to the practical use of the triangle in architecture, engineering and joinery ever being made in the mathematics classroom.

In his hotel accommodation Big George kept full sets of cricket equipment: bats, balls, gloves, pads stumps and bails which, after school hours in the summer term, were carried to the playing field by senior pupils whom George had selected as his assistants. There the boys were coached in the techniques of batting, bowling and fielding and there George divided us into teams who played matches under his supervision. On rare occasions George arranged a special treat by selecting two teams to play a cricket match at Machrihanish, about five miles from Campbeltown. He instructed the hotel staff to prepare a picnic of sandwiches, biscuits and soft drinks which was collected by the senior boys along with the cricket equipment and carried to the small local train which departed from the pier-head bound for Machrihanish. As I cannot recall being required to make any contribution towards the cost of the train fare or the food, I can only conclude that Big George met all the expenses of these outings because of his enthusiasm for cricket and his eagerness to teach the boys the rudiments of the game. The fact that these rare treats remain so firmly in my memory is testimony to the paucity of extracurricular activities and the almost uniform dullness of the fare offered in our secondary school.

In retrospect I am confident that during the later years of my secondary education the teacher who had most influence on me and best succeeded in stimulating my interest was our Principal Teacher of English, Mr. Banks, generally known as Sandy. Here was a man of scholarship and sensitivity who obviously relished his subject and was eager to encourage his pupils to share his pleasure in the beauty, riches and almost infinite variety of literature, and by frequent practice to enhance their skill in the use of the spoken and written language. He was the teacher with whom I had the greatest empathy and with whom I was able to develop as a senior pupil a positive and relaxed relationship. When I later went up to university I began to appreciate how much I had gained from his lively, inspirational teaching, his obvious enjoyment of good writing, his efforts to improve our taste and discrimination, to distinguish between the enduring and the trivial and to widen the scope of our reading, which was of special value to one like me who had been brought up in a rural parish without a public library service, and in a household where time for reading was limited by long hours of farm labour and books were accorded a low priority.

By the end of the fifth year of our secondary course most of the pupils in my class had left school, some to proceed to university or other centres of higher education, others to enter employment, and only four boys were left to embark on the sixth year of the course. For me this proved to be by far the most enjoyable year in secondary school. As it happened that all four boys in the sixth year had to stay in lodgings during the week and returned home only at weekends, we had ample opportunity to meet in the evenings, to share social activities, to enjoy evening walks and even more to enjoy endless talk and discussion of absorbing topics. Being such a small class we gradually became aware that at least some of our teachers had begun to treat us as students rather than pupils and accorded us a measure of freedom which we had not hitherto enjoyed in school. Having passed on the higher grade in five subjects in fifth year, including Greek which I had begun studying in fourth year, and having gained dux medals in all the main subjects except Mathematics, the sixth year for me was a year of relaxed study and pursuit of wider interests.

The Head of the French Department was a lively character who to us seemed middle-aged but had probably not reached the age of forty. He looked like a boxer because of his strong physique, his confident bearing and a nose that was slightly out of plumb. On a Friday afternoon which I recall he entered our classroom and regarded us with a slight grin on his face. He looked quizzically at my friend Jock who had a shock of strong, dark hair and a dark stubble on cheeks and chin which cried out for the use of a razor, but Jock kept his razor at home and shaved only at weekends. 'Galbraith', said our teacher, 'on the first occasion that I went into a shop to buy a razor, the man behind the counter looked at me and said: "What do you want a razor for; do you intend to cut your throat?"' I bet, Galbraith, he would not have said that to you!' After which pronouncement he set us an exercise to translate into French a passage from an essay by Charles Lamb.

During my time as a pupil the Grammar School did not possess a school library, but in the classroom occupied by Mr. Banks there was a small collection of English classics through which, in the sixth year, we occasionally had time to browse. I recall our delight on discovering at the back of a cupboard a complete edition of the Canterbury Tales. As our acquaintance with Chaucer had previously been confined to the prologue to the Canterbury Tales, some of the tales came as a shock and a thrill of excitement, especially to me and my closest friend, Archie, the son of our parish minister, both of us having derived our ideas about human sexual activity from reading 'good' books. In retrospect I find my own naivety and relative innocence the more difficult to understand because I had been familiar, from an early age, with the mating of the farm animals from the cats to the cattle and horses, had frequently watched them give birth and had actively helped cows deliver calves and ewes deliver lambs. I had also had ample experience in the farm stable of listening to some of the hired men and their friends boasting of their conquests and sexual prowess, yet for some unaccountable reason the reality and frequency of sexual activity outside marriage did not make much impression on me. An incident during my fourth year at secondary school remains in my memory because of the humiliation it caused me at the time. A group of my classmates who met in the evenings were talking about girls when someone raised a titter by referring to a 'french letter'. As the response to the term obviously meant something which I failed to understand I sought an explanation, only to be met with a roar of laughter and incredulity that I could be so ignorant. My standing in the group was obviously lowered for the rest of the evening and I was made the butt of further tomfoolery.

An episode on which I look back with no pride took place towards the end of my fifth year when I escorted a girl home from a party which the pupils themselves had organised. When I rather timidly kissed her goodnight she drew me close to her and insisted on kissing me properly. She then suggested that I take her to a place surrounded by a hedge which she said was used by a girl whom she knew and her boyfriend. Suffused by feelings of shyness and prudery I made an excuse that my landlady insisted on having the door locked at a certain time and made my escape. I am sure the girl must have concluded that I was an utterly useless specimen.

During my years in secondary school, as in primary school,

the most absorbing and formative experiences occurred outside school: among my school chums, in the local community and at home on the farm over weekends and school holidays. As some of my classmates and I stayed in lodgings during the school week, we formed the nucleus of a gang which some of the town-dwellers gladly joined to plan and explore ways of enjoying the evening hours, in an era when the radio, or wireless as we called it, was still uncommon and television was a diversion of the future. From late Spring until Autumn, while daylight lasted and the weather was favourable we spent much of our time playing football and other team games, or strolling in small groups towards the outskirts of the town absorbed in argument, discussion, occasional squabbles and trials of strength in bouts of rather unskilled wrestling. The standards of conduct maintained by the group must have been reasonably civilised; for I cannot recall, even in the most strenuous conflicts, any member inflicting more than minor injury on any other member of the group.

When winter weather and darkness curtailed our physical activities out-of-doors, a smaller group became attached to a gymnasium near the pier-head which was managed by a pleasant young man on behalf of the YMCA. At that time, mainly as a result of my labours on the farm, I had greater muscular development for my age than most of my pals and enjoyed gymnastic exercises on horizontal and parallel bars and on climbing-ropes and rings. At home one of my favourite sports was travelling the length of the barn by swinging like a monkey from the crossbeams near the roof. The strength built up by such pastimes and by regular work on the farm made it easy for me to climb a rope using only my hands and with my legs almost at right angles. Unfortunately, when exercises involved somersaults or a fine sense of balance I proved inferior to most of my pals, for I was afflicted with a nervous system which made me giddy even by swinging for any length of time on a child's swing and made me fall down if I pirouetted for more than a few seconds. The same weakness has made me all my life extremely liable to travel sickness.

During my period at school and later at University the cinema, with its black and white films and with no competition from such later attractions as bingo, television and video, was a much more pervasive and popular form of entertainment than it has been in recent years. In the town and surrounding district amateur dramatic clubs had not yet become popular as they did later in the century and amateur music making tended to be choral rather than orchestral, because orchestral instruments were expensive and instrumental tutors, other than teachers of piano or bagpipes, were practically unknown in the countryside. Throughout my primary and secondary education I cannot recall ever attending a live dramatic or orchestral performance, whereas concerts were held in every local hall and generally attracted an appreciative audience.

For those living in country towns and rural districts the cinema provided an attractive and affordable form of entertainment, and its weekly changing programmes generally ensured full houses, which made the cinema one of the more prosperous of local businesses. Although not all the members of our gang could afford to visit the cinema every week, we did attend as often as we could and worshipped our favourites among the film stars who to us were the glamourous stuff of dreams and sources of endless discussion. The film stars of that era enjoyed the advantage of not having to compete with the myriad stars of modern music in its various forms, nor did they have to compete with the wealth of talented performers in entertainment and sport who now fill our television screens from all over the world by day and night. Because our idols were fewer in number and appeared to live in a world of glamour and wealth so far removed from our own, perhaps our worship of them was all the more intense.

By no means all of my experiences were redolent of the artificial and fabulous life of the cinema, especially my experiences in the far from glamorous life on the farm, much as I enjoyed returning home at weekends and holidays. My Christmas holiday experience was rather different from the normal because my father had been brought up in a family which paid no attention to Christmas, as the religious sect to which my grandfather belonged regarded Christmas as a frivolous and pagan festival, and Christmas was treated as a normal working day. After the death of my mother the children were not encouraged to expect a visit from Santa Claus; members of the family did not exchange Christmas gifts; Christmas cards were not sent and very few received and the work of the farm continued on Christmas day as on any other working day.

The evening of Hogmanay was regarded as a suitable occasion for merriment and for inter-family visits with a bottle of whisky in the pocket, although my father was more inclined to receive visitors than to go out visiting on Hogmanay. It was an evening when my father took his fiddle from the shelf and kept family and visitors regaled with traditional songs and music at intervals until midnight or beyond. Occasionally the kitchen was cleared for Scottish dancing and square dances like quadrilles, lancers, petronella, flowers of Edinburgh, and various reels, with music provided by the fiddle and any visitor with an accordion or mouth-organ. One of the few accomplishments which my father tried to teach his children was traditional Scottish dancing, which was probably a reflection of a passion of his own youth, and through his tuition we all learned how to perform a wide range of country dances which, I regret to admit, I have long forgotten.

New Year's Day was one of the few days in the year which my father observed as a holiday, in that the normal work of the farm was suspended, apart from the care and feeding of livestock and the milking of cows. If the weather permitted my father's favourite way of spending the day was to have a rabbit-shoot, with the use of ferrets to bolt the rabbits from their burrows. As he did not keep ferrets on the farm, it was necessary to borrow them from a rabbit catcher or other person in the neighbourhood who kept ferrets. The collection of ferrets from a shepherd on a remote hill farm resulted in one of my few serious accidents.

On the occasion which I vividly recall I was perhaps thirteen or fourteen when my father sent me on Hogmanay to collect two ferrets from a hill farm some four or five miles distant on the road to the Mull of Kintyre. Although I was well aware that more than half the journey took me up steep hills, I pleaded with my elder sister to let me have her rather aged bicycle and, with a canvas bag on my back to hold the ferrets, I set off blithely on my errand. If I had not been foolhardy I should have left the cycle at the foot of the steep hills and walked the rest of the journey; but I insisted on pushing the old bicycle up the hills even though I had to walk the greater part of the distance.

In course of such visits in my youth it was regarded as unmannerly to refuse some form of hospitality, so I enjoyed a large cup of tea with shortbread while trying to answer the flow of questions from the shepherd, who then placed the two ferrets in my shoulder bag and sent me on my way. The downhill journey on the bicycle was enjoyable and exciting because of the speed, the uneven surface of the road, the cold wind on my face and the element of risk of which I was aware but chose to ignore with all the confidence of youth. Unfortunately I forgot that the final downhill stretch was quite steep with a right-angled bend at the bottom. On the crucial hill the brakes failed to hold; I tried without success to reduce speed by putting my right foot up on the front tyre; the speed was such that I failed to turn the final corner; the front wheel hit the road verge and I was catapulted over the handlebars into the craggy surface of a dry-stone dyke.

For how long I lay semiconscious I do not know but when I finally tottered to my feet my whole body was stiff and sore, my hands and knees were lacerated, my vision was blurred with blood, breathing was difficult and blood was dripping from my face. Luckily for me the ferrets in the canvas bag, which was still slung around my neck, were alive and seemed to be uninjured. Leaving the mangled bicycle I found my way to the nearest cottage where the housewife who responded to my kick on the door almost fainted at the sight of the bloody and swollen mask of my face. When she recovered she welcomed me in and acted very promptly by sending a message to the nearby mansion house which had a telephone. The lady of the estate acted equally promptly by providing a car with chauffeur to take me to our family doctor for emergency treatment and then to take me home. For once I received sympathy rather than blame for my escapade, although my sister mourned the loss of her bicycle.

In summary the injuries to my face comprised cut eyebrows, blackened eyes, severely injured nose, cut and bruised lips, several broken teeth and a badly cut chin. Fortunately my skull was undamaged. The only really troublesome feature proved to be my nose which was broken at the bridge, had the septum completely severed, and a deep cut over the nostrils which left the point of my nose hanging loose. I was fortunate not to lose the end of my nose altogether. Our family doctor assumed responsibility for my treatment; stuffed my nostrils with strips of lint, but for some reason did not insert stitches in the severed septum, which was held in place only with sticking plaster. At weekly intervals the doctor replaced the strips of lint which were so saturated with mucus and so sticky that the septum was again broken when the strips were withdrawn from the nostrils. As a result of this treatment it took many weeks for the septum to heal and I was left with a permanent droop to my nose which is not a handsome feature. Much more irritating and annoying; ever since that injury in my early teens I have for the rest of my life been afflicted with chronic rhinitis, which entails the frequent use of a handkerchief at all times and seasons but especially out-of-doors in cold weather.

A few years later I suffered another minor injury which involved a bicycle. A group of my classmates, boys and girls, planned an outing to Dunaverty beach, near my home, on a summer Saturday. While the majority came by bus, carrying supplies for a picnic, two boys cycled from Campbeltown. When it was discovered that milk had been omitted, one of the cyclists offered to get it from a dairy farm and, since I knew the farmer and his family, I volunteered to go with him. He had on the rear wheel of his bicycle a stubby back-step on which I balanced with one foot and my hands on his shoulders. As he increased speed his bicycle bumped over a small pothole in the road, my foot slipped and I was thrown on to the road. Although my shoulder felt numb, I again mounted on the back-step of the bicycle and we managed to reach the village before the pain became so intolerable that I had to dismount. Fortunately our family doctor was in his surgery and after examination he diagnosed a fractured collar bone. He then found that the broken ends were out of alignment and that one end had punctured the flesh, although it had not quite emerged through the skin. With some difficulty he succeeded in realigning the broken bones, put a pad under my armpit, strapped the upper arm and supported the arm with a sling. After a short rest I was able to walk the two miles home but, due to my stupidity, the girls in particular could not enjoy the picnic and the party was cut short.

Towards the end of the sixth year of my secondary course I spent a week in Glasgow taking the examinations in the Glasgow University Bursary Competition. It is evidence of the confined and narrow life which I had led that this was the first occasion on which I had travelled as far as Glasgow. During that week I stayed on the Southern outskirts of Glasgow with a family who were distantly related to my father and travelled to and from the University by tramcar. It proved to be a week of misery, for I was suffering from nervous tension, and I made the mistake of sitting on the upper deck of the tramcar which rocked its way for several miles across Glasgow with the sun (unusually for Glasgow) intensifying the overheated, overcrowded atmosphere. As a result I arrived each morning in the examination hall afflicted with travel sickness and severe headache.

In the four subjects which I had selected: English, French. Latin and Mathematics the questions were generally within my grasp, with the notable exception of the second paper in Mathematics, which dealt with topics most of which I had not been taught. I should think that I scored less than thirty per cent in that paper. Had I chosen instead to take a paper in Greek (which one of my classmates later showed me) I am confident that my performance would have been much improved. After the results were published, one of my teachers told me that the school staff had confidently expected my name to appear in the first ten, whereas it did not appear even in the first twenty. The result did, however, gain me a bursary of thirty-five pounds a year for three years.

In addition to the university bursary I gained another two competitive bursaries and was awarded a bursary by the local education authority, which placed me in the happy position of having an annual income from bursaries of one hundred and thirty pounds when I embarked on my University course in the Autumn of 1930. Although that modest sum would be regarded by the modern student as inadequate for pocket money, in the nineteen thirties it was more than many working men earned in a year, and I found that I could live on it comfortably for the three terms of the university session. During the period when the university was not in session I lived at home, in receipt of free board and lodging, but spending most of the time as an unpaid farm labourer.

Chapter 9
University Capers

MY CLOSE FRIEND ARCHIE and I, who had gone through primary and secondary school together, went up to Glasgow University together where Archie's older brother, Angus, was well on the way to completing a degree in the faculty of Arts. Throughout his University course Angus had lodged in a Church of Scotland Students' residence in Oakfield Avenue, a few minutes walk from the main University building, and Archie and I were fortunate to secure places in the same hostel, which gave priority to students who intended to study for the ministry of the Church but offered vacant places to students in other faculties. During my period as a student the Residence accommodated a healthy mixture of students in the faculties of Arts, Divinity, Law, Medicine and Science, and an occasional student who was studying at the University part-time while in employment.

My friend, Archie, who came from an academic background was quite clear that he had come up to University to read for a degree with honours in English and proceeded to fulfil his ambition. He then took a course of training as a teacher and went straight into employment as a teacher in Dunoon Grammar School in his home county of Argyll. His direct and clear progression into what he found to be a satisfying career proved to be in marked contrast with my own muddled and misguided years of University study. In the event I found myself in attendance at University either as a full-time or a part-time student for nine out of ten years between 1930 and 1940.

If I had felt confident that my father would be in a position to supplement the income which I derived from bursaries I should have applied for admission to the faculty of Medicine, which entailed five years of study and was more costly than a course in the faculty of Arts, but I was hesitant to make any demand on his small income. If I had felt an urge to teach I should have joined my friend, Archie, in reading for an honours degree in English; but as a secondary pupil I must have been rather a weird type, for I was frequently inclined to feel sorry for my teachers, faced as they were with a minority of pupils whose main objective was to waste the time and try the patience of the teacher. I had been brought up and trained by a father who treated time-wasting and incivility with equal severity.

As I had no obvious talent and little scholastic or vocational urge, my course of study was decided largely by a chance circumstance. My father knew a gentleman with family connections in Kintyre who was senior partner in a small legal firm in Glasgow, and who informed my father in conversation that if I cared to study Law he would assure me of an apprenticeship and an appointment with his firm. I therefore embarked on a three-year degree in Arts with a view to adding a degree in Law, to be completed in course of an apprenticeship.

In course of my three-year ordinary degree I attended nine classes in seven subjects, doubling in English and Latin, and including two classes which counted towards the eight required for a degree in Law. Although I tried to reserve some part of each day for study and gained four first class and three second class certificates, including a prize in French for class work, there still seemed to be ample time for recreation and leisure pursuits. Having from childhood enjoyed running I joined the University Athletic Club and spent several hours each week practising middle-distance running at Westerlands, the university sports ground. Through the Athletic Club I became acquainted with a number of people who gained prominence in Scottish and international athletics. Keen as I was my ability in athletics was mediocre, and the highest level which I reached was occasionally representing the University as a 'second string' in 440 and 880 yards events at inter- university sports.

My friend Archie joined the University Football Section and there achieved the distinction of playing at back for the University first team. His partner at back was also a tall, handsome young man named Norman Stone who occasionally sat beside me in University classes. After the passage of almost sixty years it is still for me a great sadness that neither of these two most promising young men survived the 1939-45 war. If ever two men enjoyed and loved life it was these two, and their untimely death epitomised for me the utter waste of war. I have never again had a friend as close as Archie.

Because of our enthusiasm for athletics Archie and I shared an experience which was rather unusual and in some respects quite ludicrous. While still at secondary school we two had eagerly assisted Archie's older brother Angus and one or two other enthusiasts in organising and running Highland Games in our native parish of Southend. As the winning athletes at these local sports received modest money prizes, not exceeding ten shillings (50p) they were counted in athletics circles as professional sports. Those of us who were keen on athletics competition had no option but to compete at Highland Games, for throughout Kintyre amateur athletics meetings were unknown. In order to meet athletes from other districts and encourage them to come as competitors to our Highland Games, four of us (Angus, Archie, another friend Hamish and I) travelled in a shared car to compete at Highland Games in various districts of Argyllshire. Our athletic success was limited, except for Hamish who became prominent at games throughout the county as a heavyweight athlete, particularly in throwing the sixteen-pound hammer.

I recall a notable occasion when the four of us spent a day at the Cowal Highland Games in Dunoon. Having left home early in the morning, and having eaten practically nothing all day, we stopped on the homeward journey at Lochgair Hotel, which was noted for the quality of the high teas which it served. We ordered a large platter of bacon with two eggs each and a generous supply of bread and cakes. When we gathered round the table and the heaped plates of food were served, the conversation died away while we attacked the food. The silence was broken by Hamish who was spreading butter on a piece of bread. 'If I just had some one to spread the butter on my bread', said he, 'I would get on a good deal faster'.

The sports provision at Glasgow University in the nineteen thirties did not quite measure up to modern standards. At Westerlands the ground was so restricted that the athletics track measured 300 yards instead of the standard 440 yards. Probably for that reason the University sports in the Summer included an event entitled the novices' 600 yards, intended for students who had not previously competed at the university sports. My friend Archie and I entered for this event and, perhaps due to our experience in Highland Games, I came in first and Archie came in second. Within two weeks of the event the Secretary of the University Athletic Club received an anonymous letter, with an Argyllshire postmark, stating that to the knowledge of the writer two professional athletes had competed at the University sports and Archie and I were named.

In due course we were summoned to appear before a panel of the University Athletic Club where we freely admitted that we had competed at Highland Games because in our district no amateur athletic meetings were held. We were given the choice of being reinstated as amateur athletes or of being barred from competition at all amateur athletic meetings, including the University sports meetings. Having chosen to be reinstated as amateurs we were summoned to appear before a panel of the Scottish Amateur Athletic Association, who duly interviewed us and finally agreed to our reinstatement as amateur athletes. The feature of the interview panel which most tickled my sense of humour was that the chairman of the panel was a prominent director of Celtic football club, one of the strongest professional sports clubs in Scotland. As my friend Archie and I indulged in athletics for the sole reason that we enjoyed it, and as we were well aware that many of the prizes in kind handed over to amateur athletes greatly exceeded in value the maximum of ten shillings which we had ever received, and which did not meet our travelling expenses, I have always looked back with cynical amusement on the mock solemnity of our reinstatement as amateur athletes. It certainly did nothing to lessen our support of our local Highland Games on the organisation and running of which we spent much time and energy during our summer vacation.

Among the group of some twenty students whom I joined in the Church of Scotland Students' Residence was a small, slightly built young man with a shock of reddish hair and a somewhat sardonic expression who was reading Classics and English. This young man, David, was in many respects the most lively and stimulating companion in residence, for he always seemed to have time for activities other than study and in many of the ploys which occupied our leisure time he was the one who took the initiative. Although I doubt whether David was a scholar in the sense of one devoted to a particular field of study, in retrospect I regard him as one of the most intelligent and quick-witted men it has been my privilege to meet: sharp of intellect and sharp of tongue and with an outstanding capacity for absorbing knowledge. He achieved without apparent effort a degree with first class honours in Classics and was obviously disappointed to miss a first class honours in English.

Among other pursuits David was attracted to games of chance and this led to my initiation into activities of which hitherto I had no experience. In the early nineteen thirties the football pools had not yet been centralised in a few national firms A bookmaking firm in Glasgow which, if my memory serves aright, was called J. John and Company ran a football competition named a 'Sunny Six' which was won by forecasting the correct results of six games selected by the promoter. In a normal week the money available for distribution was shared among a number of people who had submitted a correct forecast and, in modern terms, individual winnings were quite modest. According to David's information, however, winnings were paid only for a completely correct forecast and, as sometimes happened, if no correct entry was received the stake money was carried forward to the following week, when the lucky winners might earn a few thousand pounds.

David paid a visit to the office of J. John where he was assured by a member of staff that the pools coupons which were published in local newspapers and were available from the office could be supplemented if required by home-made coupons. Fortified by this assurance he then took the trouble to calculate the permutations on the Sunny Six and recorded the details on sheets of paper. After intensive canvassing he recruited about ten students from the Residence who were prepared to help in making many hundreds of copies of the coupons and, more important, were prepared to contribute about fourteen pounds each towards the total entry fee. In those days fourteen pounds was a considerable sum which none of us could readily afford and it was a tribute to David's confidence and persuasive tongue that he found so many financial backers for his gamble. We then waited patiently until a week occurred when David learned that J. John had paid no dividend, and for some days during the following week we spent all our leisure time completing coupons from the list of permutations. A number of us used our home address, while a few used the Residence as their address. The completed coupons were then handed in and we awaited the outcome. In the event we had an all-correct coupon, but we could only conclude that it must have been an easy week when too many other correct entries were submitted, for the total dividend which we received was about twenty-five pounds less than the total cost of entry, and we each suffered a loss of between two and three pounds. That taught us a salutary lesson although it did not completely cure us of the urge to gamble.

After licking our wounds and following lengthy discussion, David decided that we were at the wrong end of the football pools business, where the real money was made by the promoters at the expense of the punters. He was strongly of the opinion that if we could raise some capital we had more than enough intelligence and capacity for organisation to establish a pools business which, with a little initial good fortune, could be expanded indefinitely. The idea was carried forward and explored to the point where we visited and inspected vacant offices in the centre of Glasgow. In the event we came up against the harsh reality that, in those days, capital could not be raised by a group of inexperienced young men unless with solid backing which none of us was in a position to provide. Reluctantly we abandoned our plans; but many years later, when David was one of the most prominent educationalists in Scotland, I reminded him of our youthful escapades and expressed the opinion that if we had succeeded in establishing a football pools business in the early nineteen thirties, with his brains and business acumen to guide us, it would almost certainly have flourished to the extent that he would be riding round Glasgow driven by a chauffeur in a Rolls Bentley.

In the summer term David found a tipster who appeared to obtain inside information from one large stable, for the horses which he tipped from that particular stable won with such consistency that some of us felt confident enough to place small each-way bets on them. Towards the end of the summer term I found myself with some cash still in the bank and bet one pound each way on a horse with an Irish name which won a selling plate race at odds of twenty to one. On the strength of that win I went into partnership with my pal Archie in buying a second-hand car for the sum of twelve pounds. The car was a Morris two-seater which had been made in 1925 and with it we ran around during the summer vacation, including visits to most of the Highland Games in Argyllshire. Archie already held a driving licence and, under his tuition, I passed my driving test at the second attempt with that old car. At the end of the summer vacation we sold it for ten pounds before returning to University.

One of David's friends was the son of a cinema manager who obtained a number of passes for the previewing of films prior to their release for public viewing in cinemas throughout Scotland. Through the good offices of his friend, David was able to obtain some of these passes, which enabled a small group of us to attend the showing of films at morning sessions in one of the cinemas in the centre of Glasgow By this means we were privileged to see, free of charge, a number of the best films from Hollywood and British studios before they were included in the film programmes of cinemas in Glasgow. We did not seem to worry unduly about cutting University lectures to enjoy the treat of previewing these films.

The Arts faculty of the University had its quota of pedestrian lecturers who did nothing to set their students alight, but fortunately the faculty, like other faculties of the University, included some outstanding personalities who made their subject come alive and whose lectures it was a pleasure and a privilege to attend. One such was the Professor of English and another the Professor of Moral Philosophy, whose lectures were frequently attended by students who were not taking the subject in their degree. It is one of my personal regrets that I opted to take Logic instead of Moral Philosophy. I recall the Professor preaching a sermon in the University chapel which lasted for forty minutes and it was not one minute too long; it was one of the most eloquent and outstanding addresses to which I have ever listened.

To me one of the most attractive personalities on the University staff was the young chaplain, Archie Craig, who later became one of the most prominent and best-loved ministers in the Church of Scotland. Largely because of the high quality of the services in the University chapel, I did not form a connection with any church in Glasgow but attended the chapel services with fair regularity.

Partly because he resided in a house in Gibson Street, immediately below the Church of Scotland Students' Residence, and partly because of that Church connection, the Rev. Archie Craig was a frequent and welcome visitor to the Residence where he maintained an interest in our progress, dispensed sound advice and exchanged banter with the students in the common room. After I left the University I did not meet Archie Craig until his year of office as Moderator of the General Assembly of the Church of Scotland, when I was Director of Education for the Combined County of Perth and Kinross. It was typical of the man that on our meeting he immediately recognised me and recalled my name.

Among the members of the Residence at that time was a handsome, fair-haired young man of athletic build who was a part-time student employed by a major insurance company. Many of his weekends were spent climbing mountains in various parts of Scotland. As he was in employment he rose and had breakfast rather earlier than some of us, but he invariably took time for a regular period of physical exercise in his bedroom before he got dressed. In summer he exercised before his open bedroom window.

One morning the Rev. Archie Craig had an early appointment and was impatiently awaiting his breakfast which failed to arrive. He finally went through to the kitchen at the rear of his house which faced the Residence, and there found his young housemaid standing at the window, gazing in fascination at a handsome young man doing his exercises stark naked in front of his bedroom window. That evening Archie had occasion to visit the Residence to have a quiet word with the young man about the advisability of his conducting his fitness exercises rather more discreetly in future, however disappointed the housemaid might be at losing her morning spectacle.

When I went up to University it was rather unusual for a student to own a car, but we had in the Residence two brothers, Andrew and John, who had acquired at very modest cost a small car which they drove for years in and around Glasgow and sometimes farther afield. As both brothers were highly skilled drivers it was a pleasure, though sometimes rather an exciting one, to be driven by one of the brothers through central Glasgow. I can still recall such a drive through some of the busiest streets in the city and cutting between two tramcars which were coming to meet each other. Towards the end of his University career the older brother fell in love with a girl who introduced him to her family. On returning to the Residence one evening he described in detail an episode which we all enjoyed. He had taken his girlfriend and her mother for a run in the little car and on the return journey, along a relatively new stretch of road known as the Knightswood boulevard, he was amazed to see a car wheel bowling along the road in front of him. A moment's reflection convinced him that the wheel must have come from his car, and when he braked and looked round there was the girlfriend's mother holding on to the sagging rear of the car. Fortunately the axle had not come in contact with the road and, on retrieving the errant wheel, he was able to refit it by using one wheel nut from each of the other three wheels and managed to motor home without further mishap.

As a result of his friendship with Angus and Archie, the sons of our parish minister, Andrew during one summer vacation drove the little car from Glasgow to Kintyre and, among other ploys, insisted on visiting the lighthouse at the Mull of Kintyre. Angus. Archie and I went with him as his passengers, but on the steepest hills the load proved too much for the little car, so two of the passengers dismounted and followed the car uphill, each carrying a large stone to block the rear wheels in the event of the car stalling and threatening to roll back down hill. Our experience of climbing the hills was such that fortunately, though with difficulty, we were able to persuade Andrew not to drive the car down the final hill, with hairpin bends, to reach the lighthouse. I am convinced that if Andrew had insisted on driving the car to the lighthouse down one of the steepest hills on a main road in Scotland, it would never have returned under its own power.

The average speed of travel by car in those days was about half of the average speed today. During one of my years at University I became friendly with an Indian student who must have come from a wealthy family, and who appeared oblivious of the relative poverty in which I had to live. Some of the places to which he took me and some of the events, including a ball in the RAC Club at which I was the only person not in full evening dress, left me feeling totally embarrassed. In course of the year he bought a new sports car which provided a standard of luxury to which I have never aspired. When as a passenger in that car I was first driven at over eighty miles per hour I thought it was a terrifying speed. Today it is commonplace.

On occasional nights out a party of students from the Residence attended a performance at the old Pavilion Theatre, which frequently put on music hall shows sustained mainly by

Scottish comedians. The best of these such as Tommy Lorne, Dave Willis and Will Fyffe were comedians of such outstanding talent that I can still enjoy the memory of their performances, and we probably did not appreciate how fortunate we were to have the privilege of watching them and listening to them in pantomimes and variety shows. Unfortunately the supporting turns were sometimes of inferior quality and were treated as such by discerning audiences. One evening a large party from the Residence attended a variety show at the Pavilion to celebrate a birthday, after those who were not abstainers had drunk a few beers at a favourite hostelry. The mood of the party was such that I was able to feel high on one glass of cider. We settled down in one of the front rows of the pavilion ready to enjoy ourselves, but the opening turn consisted of two so-called comedians who fully deserved the cold silence which pervaded the house. Among our number was Ian from Portree who gave a bellow of laughter at some derogatory remark made by his neighbour, and immediately we could see the eyes of the duo on the stage swivelling on to him. This caused the whole party from the Residence, in their lubricated condition, to begin laughing and within minutes the whole theatre was lit up with laughter. It was a striking example of the infectious power of laughter, for even the comedians seemed to improve under its influence, as from then on we thoroughly enjoyed the show.

Towards the end of the third year of my University course, which I had greatly enjoyed, I was compelled to face up to serious problems some of which I should have foreseen, although my difficulties were aggravated by events that I could not have anticipated. My problems began with the unexpected death of the man who had promised me a place in his legal firm. For the first time I began canvassing legal firms for an apprenticeship and was appalled to find, as I should have been aware, that the standard pay for an apprentice was ten shillings (50p) per week. Further more I was informed by a partner in one large firm that their senior assistant, who had been a qualified solicitor for some time, was earning only three pounds per week. This posed for me a serious difficulty, in that as a law apprentice I should have to lodge in Glasgow for fifty weeks, while as a University student I had to pay boarding fees for only thirty weeks in the year. As an apprentice in law I should also have to dress more smartly and more expensively than as a student.

My second unforeseen difficulty arose from a serious outbreak of brucellosis in my father's dairy herd. The outcome of this widespread disease was that the small profit which he normally made on his farming operations was turned into a loss, which continued for two or three years and left the whole family in a precarious situation. In these circumstances I could not possibly expect any financial contribution from my father to the cost of my education and training in Glasgow. My financial problems were greatly aggravated by the fact that the bursaries on which I had lived comfortably throughout my course all terminated at the end of three years, and I could anticipate a situation in which I had no income and would be compelled to return home to the family farm.

The future seemed so bleak that I think for a period I suffered from a kind of a personal breakdown when, for the first and only time in my life, I became obsessed with my weaknesses and the fear of complete failure. During my period in primary and secondary school self-doubt rarely obtruded, because I was always first in my class and, though physically slight, I could hold my own at most physical activities. At secondary school so little importance was attached to Art and Music that my artistic and musical deficiencies could be ignored. Only when I went up to University did I find that in every subject there were students of greater ability, aptitude and application than I possessed. In many ways that discovery was good for me as it acted as an incentive but, as I grew older, I became conscious of qualities other than intellectual which were important for a satisfying life and in which I failed to measure up to most of my companions.

One of my persistent worries centred on what I had come to regard as my hair-trigger nervous system which made me hyper-sensitive to a variety of physical and social stimuli. I have previously referred to an extreme tendency to giddiness which, as I grew older, also included a fear of heights, although as a child I had no such fear in climbing to the tops of high trees, clambering over the pitched roofs of the farm steading and swinging from the high crossbeams along the length of the barn. When travelling by steamer as I frequently did between Campbeltown and Gourock I found that I was always the first among my fellows to suffer from seasickness and there are few experiences that give one a more debilitating sense of inferiority than to feel desperately ill when all one's friends are enjoying themselves. I had developed a tendency to lose control of my temper on rather slight provocation and on these occasions I had an almost irresistible urge to resort to physical violence which, fortunately, I was able to conceal. In pathetic contrast I suffered from chronic rhinitis. Although I had not at any time failed an examination, I had become increasingly anxious about my ability to succeed.

Through the generosity and advice of two good men my financial dilemma was at least partially resolved. My friend David, who was a keen student of the University Calendar, had discovered details of a bursary entitled the Mary Allan Bell bursary which was awarded on examination to a student in the faculty of Divinity, Law or Medicine and amounted to £50 annually. David had succeeded in gaining this bursary and held it for two years on the strength of taking two subjects in Law. On David's advice I entered the competition and was awarded the bursary which gave me an income of fifty pounds for each of the following three years.

In the late nineteen twenties my older brother Donald emigrated to Southern Rhodesia (now Zimbabwe) where Uncle Donald Black was a prosperous farmer and had offered my brother a position as trainee manager on his farm. Uncle Donald had also informed his nephew that, after training, he could obtain a lease of land on favourable terms from the Government, who wished to encourage the settlement of young farmers from Britain. It happened that Donald returned to Kintyre for his first period of leave just at the time of my most urgent financial difficulty. When about to return to Rhodesia he found that he had some surplus cash and, on learning of my dilemma, he insisted on giving me more than two hundred pounds, which proved to be the most valuable assistance which I have received in my lifetime. This most welcome relief to my poverty, though not enough to enable me to complete an apprenticeship in Law, did enable me to plan for two more years at University.

Although not so averse to the choice of teaching as I had been on entering University, I still preferred to explore other avenues. In the hope of gaining a qualification for a career in commerce or industry my first thought was to take the degree of Bachelor of Commerce, but that would have entailed a change of university and loss of my £50 bursary. As I had taken, in my third year, classes in Economics and history the rather confused plan which I adopted was to complete a degree with honours in Economics and History, while at the same time seeking to complete the degree of Ll. B. I therefore embarked on a heavy programme of study in my fourth year: taking Higher Economics, Higher History and Scottish Economic History and adding Civil Law, Constitutional Law and History and Public International Law towards a degree in Law. By the end of the session I had passed the degree examinations in these subjects. In my fifth year at University I took five subjects: Economics and History in the Faculty of Arts; the Law of Scotland, Evidence and Procedure and Jurisprudence in the Faculty of Law. By passing the degree examinations in the three subjects in Law I qualified for the degree of Ll. B, although I readily admit that it was largely a paper qualification.

Unfortunately I had reached another crisis in my endeavour to take an honours degree in Arts. Although I had obtained a Certificate of Distinction in History and was encouraged by a member of the lecturing staff to pursue the subject, I failed to secure a Certificate of Distinction in Economics and, more disturbing, when I embarked on a study of the Treatise on Money by Keynes, and other publications in the more advanced field of economics, I became convinced that the subject at that level was too abstruse and mathematical for a student like me who was endowed with little talent in Logic or Mathematics. After brooding over the problem, I concluded that to spend another year on even more advanced study and perhaps secure a third class or a poor second class degree was more than I could bear. Having in my ignorance followed for five years a thoroughly botched and muddled course of University study, which involved attendance at precisely twenty classes and a range of reading such as few students can have attempted, I resolved to abandon it and put it behind me. As it was now imperative to gain some professional qualification that would enable me to earn my living, I finally bit the bullet and applied for admission in the following session to Jordanhill College to train as a teacher.

Chapter 10
A Brief Career

AFTER FIVE YEARS AT University my financial position was again becoming precarious, for my father was still in no position to give me an allowance. It occurred to me that if I could attend two classes in Law during my year of training at Jordanhill College, that would qualify me to retain the Mary Allan Bell bursary of fifty pounds, which would partially relieve my financial difficulty. I therefore matriculated for a sixth year and arranged to attend a class in Law at eight o'clock in the morning, before hastening to Jordanhill by bus to engage in my course of training as a teacher. It was also necessary to attend in the late afternoon a class which could be included in a Law degree and there I met with a problem. The only late afternoon class which I had not previously attended was the subject of Accountancy, which was attended mainly by trainee accountants. The lectures were pitched at a level which assumed that the students had been employed for some time in an accountancy or legal firm and knew how to prepare a straightforward set of company accounts, whereas I was entirely ignorant of even the simplest form of bookkeeping. The lecturer also gave the students lengthy exercises in Accountancy to do at weekends. As I knew none of the students I could not ask for assistance; it was a constant struggle just to keep in touch with the work of the class, and in order to secure a 'duly performed' certificate I was compelled to devote more time and effort to that one subject than I did to all the subjects which were included in my course at Jordanhill. The combination of University and College classes demanded such long hours of concentrated study that I had little time for recreation, and I was relieved at the end of the session to receive a certificate of

'Very Promising' as a teacher and a mark of 'Excellent' for teaching practice. I had also gained my bursary for attendance at two classes in Law. More important was the discovery that I actually enjoyed teaching children.

In the mid nineteen thirties, when I qualified as a teacher, there always seemed to be more young teachers emerging from the training colleges than there were teaching vacancies to be filled. As this situation of oversupply of teachers had prevailed for years, it was an important factor in contributing to the low esteem accorded to the profession in general. It also placed the education authorities and their administrative officers in a very powerful position to select only those young teachers whom they wished to employ, and to dictate the terms and conditions of their employment. Tales abounded of young teachers who emerged from the training colleges with an indifferent report from the Principal only to spend years vainly seeking employment, or offered merely part-time employment to fill temporary vacancies when serving teachers were absent from duty. A few years before I qualified the notorious 'Geddes Axe' had sliced a percentage from the salaries of all serving teachers, and the bitterness which that caused was still apparent among experienced teachers in the schools in which I served. From the date on which the Geddes Axe fell teachers received no increase in their salary scales until 1945. Morale was not helped by the regulation that, when a woman teacher married, her contract of service was automatically terminated, even though the application of the rule created vacancies for young women teachers. Many of the married men teachers with whom I served vowed that they would strongly advise their children not to choose teaching as a career.

When I qualified as a teacher Glasgow Education Authority paid their teachers on a somewhat higher scale than did other education authorities in Scotland. Probably for that reason the Authority could fill vacancies so easily that applications were not accepted from newly-qualified teachers who came from areas other than Glasgow, unless the applicant had received from the training college a 'Very Promising' estimate as a teacher. As I appeared to be one of the more promising teachers emerging from Jordanhill College in 1936 my application for employment in Glasgow was accepted, and within six weeks of qualifying I received a telegram instructing me to report to a junior secondary school on the east end of Glasgow. My most enduring memories of class 2E in that school are the smell of wet coats hung on pegs along one wall of the classroom and the problem of dealing with two boys who had acquired a supply of carpet-tacks which they expertly threw at other boys across the room immediately my back was turned.

After a few weeks in that testing environment I was handed in mid-morning another telegram instructing me to report in the afternoon of that day to North Kelvinside Senior Secondary School, where I was required to teach Geography and Latin, in neither of which I held a qualification, although I had fortunately studied Latin for two years at University. From there after a few weeks I was sent to a junior instruction centre, where unemployed youth were kept occupied in such elementary education and training activities as the members of staff could devise. As the ability of the boys ranged from the quite bright to the very dull, it was far from easy to keep all the lads occupied and interested. The main weapon for maintaining some semblance of discipline was to exclude the more rebellious members from attending the class. Those who were excluded were reported to the employment centre (known as 'The Buroo') which promptly cancelled the payment of unemployment benefit. The youngster was then probably assaulted by his parents or thrown out of his home because he brought home no money, and unless he was a very tough character he would give up and seek readmission to the junior instruction centre.

One of my more vivid memories is of finding at the centre a boy who had failed to memorise the alphabet. This I discovered when I asked the boys to find the meaning of some words selected from a passage of reading by looking up the meaning in small dictionaries which were among our tiny supply of books. On seeing one boy turning the pages of the dictionary at random, I asked him to go through the alphabet and was amazed when he stuck at the letter 'g'. When I asked him to start again he stuck at the same letter, then hung his head and said in a pathetic voice: 'Ach Goad, Sir, Ah've forgot'. He was a pleasant lad and I could not but feel pity for him.

Following these brief periods of varied experience, which were probably not untypical of the unthinking way in which officials of the Authority threw newly-qualified teachers in at 'the deep end', I was fortunate enough to be given a permanent posting to a primary school in the district of Maryhill. This suited me perfectly as the school was within easy walking distance of the University, and I was eager to resume University studies at the earliest opportunity. My satisfaction at securing employment in Glasgow was based on the knowledge that the Education Authority had adopted a policy of granting teachers permission to attend within school hours university classes leading to the degree of Bachelor of Education (now entitled Master of Education) . The degree was in two parts: a diploma stage and an honours stage. By agreement between Glasgow University and Jordanhill Training College, students in training were allowed to attend the university for the diploma stage of the degree by taking classes in Education and Psychology at the University instead of taking the same classes at Jordanhill. For me this had not been practicable because of the classes I was already taking at University. I was therefore faced with the task of studying for both stages of the degree on a part-time basis while engaged in full-time teaching.

My eagerness to take the higher degree in Education and Psychology was strengthened by my awareness that my career prospects in teaching were limited by my lack of an honours degree, which was essential for teaching senior classes and gaining promotion in a secondary school. I was also aware that the degree of Ed. B. was one of the accepted qualifications for appointment as an educational psychologist, and that a combination of the degrees of Ll. B. and Ed. B. could qualify a teacher for an appointment on the administrative side of education. I therefore applied and was granted permission by Glasgow Education Authority to attend university classes on a part-time basis from the beginning of session 1937-38. Such permission was granted on condition that for classes attended during school hours salary would be deducted for the duration of the class plus thirty minutes for travelling time. In consequence my gross salary of two hundred and twenty five pounds as a primary teacher was reduced to about one hundred and eighty pounds on which I found that I could just survive. Study for the degree of Ed. B., added to the preparatory work which I considered essential as an inexperienced teacher in order to do justice to my primary class, left me with practically no time for recreation, except on Saturday afternoons which I generally devoted to long-distance running with the Hares and Hounds section of the University Athletic Club. As I did not consider myself to be among the most talented members of the team selected to run for the University, I am inclined to think that the University 'Blue' which I was awarded was as much for long service as for ability. While I found that long-distance running was an enjoyable social activity and a good way of maintaining physical fitness, long-distance racing was quite another matter and, in my opinion, a pursuit suitable only for masochists.

When I settled down in my primary school I became increasingly aware of the wealth of teaching talent which Glasgow Education Authority at that time employed in its primary schools. I found that most of the teachers in our school were of a very high standard in their personal qualities, in their devotion to their profession, in their teaching ability and their interest in the welfare of their pupils. Although the classrooms were sparsely furnished with dual desks and seats firmly fixed to the floor, with none of the modern teaching aids, with a limited range of textbooks and with pupils of a wide spread of ability in classes often exceeding forty, the standard of attainment from infant to senior classes was in general highly satisfactory. In the large primary schools which were normal in Glasgow, the great majority of women teachers could not at that time expect any promotion but had to be content with the status of assistant teacher throughout their career and when, by annual increments not exceeding ten pounds, they reached the top of their salary scale, their salary remained unaltered from year to year for the rest of their teaching life. The accepted posts of responsibility for women teachers were Infant Mistress and Senior Woman Assistant: the one responsible for the organisation and supervision of infant classes and the other holding a special responsibility for the welfare of girls in the junior and senior classes. The men teachers who comprised about a quarter of the staff in a large primary school could compete for promotion to posts as Second Master and then as Headmaster. In the nineteen thirties promotion to these posts under Glasgow Education Authority was at least in part a reward for long service, and I formed the impression that promotion often came too late in a teacher's career for the good of the individual concerned and still more for the good of the school. There was a tendency for a headmaster who was appointed towards the end of his career to be content to sit in the headmaster's room, leaving the other promoted staff to supervise and run the school. I can recall my headmaster visiting my classroom only once during my period of service in the school, although it was my first permanent appointment, including two years as a probationary teacher.

From the other men teachers on the staff, who were highly experienced and taught only senior classes, I received more sound advice and guidance and far more consideration and kindness than I had any right to expect. Even after it became known in the school that I had applied for permission to attend university classes on a part-time basis, and would be absent from duty for certain periods during the university session, none of the men or women teachers ever complained that my classes had to be supervised during my absence, nor did any member of staff ever display resentment at my upstart ambition. As a teacher on probation I was given a primary 4 class which I was expected to retain for three years until I passed the class over to a senior teacher at primary 7 stage. This arrangement had the advantage that the ability of a young teacher to bring a class to a satisfactory standard of attainment could be assessed over a three-year period.

The advice which I received from my senior colleagues was to maintain discipline very firmly even with a junior class, until my confidence was established and the pupils recognised that I was not the kind of teacher with whom they could take liberties. This I did for perhaps longer than was necessary, for I was fortunate to have a class, albeit of very mixed ability, which contained no exhibitionist and no rogue element. Apart from one incident my life in school flowed from week to week with pleasing smoothness. In course of my second year of probation the school received a visit from H. M. Inspectors, and the Inspector assigned to my class was young and perhaps relatively inexperienced with primary pupils. At the end of his inspection he offered me no advice and no criticism, but he did ask if I had met any difficulties in my teaching. I replied that I had not so far encountered any serious problem but that I was not entirely satisfied with the standard of neatness in the handwriting of a few pupils, and that perhaps he could offer me some advice on the teaching of handwriting. I received no advice but, when H. M. Inspectors' report was received by the headmaster, one of the few specific criticisms was that the standard of handwriting in my primary 5 class could be improved. That was the occasion when I received my only classroom visit from the Headmaster who obviously felt that I had let the side down. He was probably the more puzzled by the end of session results for the Second Master was pleased to let me know that the average scores made by my class in the term examinations were uniformly higher than in the other classes at the same stage, which had been taught by experienced teachers. It took many years to restore my confidence in the worth of H. M. Inspectors of schools.

When I felt sufficiently confident and relaxed with my class, we began to leaven the normal routine of classwork with such lighter activities as I thought might interest the children. On recalling the pleasure which I had gained from the songs that I had been taught in primary school I decided that, despite the handicap of my relative illiteracy in Music, we should have a period of class singing at least once a week. In the absence of song-books the words had to be written on the blackboard, and without a piano I had to sing the tune at a pitch which I hoped would be suitable for children's voices. Despite the difficulties our singing sessions were greatly enjoyed, and I learned later that they were heard with envy by the class on the other side of the partition. The children also looked forward to the stories which I told or read to them, especially as I encouraged them to laugh aloud at any humorous episode, until laughter became an accepted feature of the class. When we had an opportunity to play games in the playground, I encouraged the boys and girls to play together at ball games, although I was aware that some of the boys were averse to allowing the girls into a game of football, keen as some of the girls were to take part.

In my second year with the class I recall making a blunder. During an afternoon session I felt that some of the pupils were beginning to take my forbearance too much for granted, and I issued a warning that the next child to cause any disturbance would be punished. As it happened the victim was the brightest and most popular girl in the class who persisted in chattering to her neighbour. I called her out to my desk and, intent on showing that I had no favourites in the class, although I rarely used the tawse I gave her two light strokes on the palm of her hand. More through chagrin than pain the tears came to her eyes, and I realised from the shocked and hostile silence of the whole class that I had been convicted of injustice and was regarded for the rest of the day as an enemy. Two days later when I emerged from the school in the afternoon two girls were waiting at the school gate: one the girl whom I had punished and the other her close friend. Without a word they ranged on either side of me and each took one of my hands to convoy me along the street.

What was I to do? I was scared of what the senior teachers would think if I were seen walking hand in hand with two of my girl pupils. Even worse if my Headmaster were informed of it. It was assuredly not how a teacher in Glasgow at that time was expected to conduct himself. But a moment's reflection told me that I simply could not reject the two girls. Their gesture was obviously a peace offering; it was their way of showing that I had been forgiven. As the girls were too shy to open a conversation I asked them about how they spent their weekends and holidays, enquired if they had brothers and sisters, and tried to learn something about their families which I had not previously been able to do.

When our ways diverged they wished me goodbye and I assumed that would be the last of the episode; but on the following afternoon the two girls again awaited me at the school gate, took my hands and on this occasion they asked me questions about myself and my family. They were particularly interested to hear about my childhood which had differed so much from their city upbringing. After a few days the two girls were joined by another two girls from the class who linked hands with the first two as we walked along practically filling the pavement. From then until the summer of 1939, when the mass evacuation of children from Glasgow was organised, I was met by a group of girls when I emerged from the school, sometimes as many as eight, when there was rivalry about who would take my hands and I was convoyed along the street, while the girls laughed and chattered like birds in springtime. I felt grateful to my colleagues on the school staff that at no time did anyone comment on my behaviour or the behaviour of the girls. Needless to say that no boy from the class ever joined the group.

Some years ago a married lady introduced herself to me and reminded me that she had been one of the girls in my primary school class in Maryhill. I was delighted to meet her and flattered that she had recognised me after a lapse of more than fifty years. In course of an animated conversation she suddenly laughed and said, to my amazement, 'We girls thought you were wonderful'. When I enquired why, she replied that it was because they had fun in my class; I had encouraged them to laugh and to sing and, best of all, in the playground I had treated the girls as equal with the boys and had allowed them to play football with the boys. On such small things apparently does the contentment of young children and their abiding memory of a teacher depend.

By 1937 those of us who took an interest in international politics were sorely perturbed by the looming danger of war. I persevered with my part-time studies in the hope that peace would last long enough to enable me to complete the honours stage of my degree in Education and Psychology. I can recall few more depressing experiences than walking along the darkened streets of Glasgow on the occasion of the first trial blackout, which presaged in the most dramatic way the horrors that were to come.

In 1939 my studies were interrupted by the evacuation of children from Glasgow. All credit to the effort expended by the authorities on this huge operation which at the time seemed fully justified, but the emotional strain imposed on the children, the parents and the families who received them in the billeting areas is beyond description. The pupils and teachers from our school, together with those parents who decided to accompany their children, boarded a train in Glasgow with no knowledge of our destination. The children carried their gas-masks and a suitcase or other container for their belongings. In the event we had a relatively easy journey as we had been assigned to the fertile farming district lying between Perth and Dundee and stretching from Kinfauns to Longforgan. At each rural station in the Carse a group of pupils, parents and teachers left the train to be met on the platform by a reception party headed by the local billeting officer. By the time we had been transported to the local school darkness had fallen. The allocation of pupils and parents to suitable billets was a time-consuming process, and it was nearly midnight when a farmer's wife and family invited me to accompany them to their farm where I was well fed and allocated a comfortable bedroom.

Because of the excitement and tension of the previous day I was unable to enjoy a restful sleep and before eight o'clock in the morning I was dressed and out in the farm close, enjoying the familiar ambience of an isolated farm but still with little knowledge of where I was in relation to Perth and Dundee. As I stood there relaxing in the peace and admiring the scenery, a woman with a suitcase and a child on each hand came walking down from a cottage located at some little distance from the farm. I recognised the children as pupils from our school and greeted the mother by asking her where she was going at that hour in the morning. 'Mr Young', she replied, 'Ah'm gaun Hame; Ah couldna live oot here in the middle o'a park!' And, despite my best efforts to dissuade her, back she went to Glasgow with her two children.

Although many of the children from Glasgow settled down and enjoyed the country life, from which they derived untold benefit educationally, physically and socially, many others, especially when accompanied by their parents, drifted back to Glasgow. The return of pupils to Glasgow proved to be of unexpected benefit to me because teachers were required to teach them and, as a part-time student, I was given priority to return to Glasgow in time to resume my university studies, and also to complete a thesis which was heavy with statistics and which was an integral part of the degree.

I was due to sit the final examination in September, 1940, but two weeks before the examination I received my call-up for military service. After seeking advice I applied for deferment of call-up for four weeks to enable me to sit the final examinations. On the day on which the examination results were published I just had time to send a telegram to my father: 'Glad to report first class honours', before boarding a train to Catterick in Yorkshire where I began military training in a tank regiment. I had received no opportunity to express a preference nor was I informed in which branch of the armed services I would be trained.

Chapter 11
Gone for a Soldier

THE TROOP IN WHICH I was placed comprised a healthy cross-section of young men, including the son of a consultant surgeon from Edinburgh, the son of a wealthy Jewish textile merchant from Manchester and two ex-borstal lads from Glasgow. Our troop instructor was a sergeant in the regular army, who rode a powerful motorcycle and looked as fit and lean as a greyhound. Under his instruction, especially on the barrack square, and with the benefit of a healthy diet and open-air life, the two lads from Glasgow visibly flourished and, by the end of their preliminary training their appearance, physique and general deportment had so improved that they showed every promise of being first-class soldiers. The tall son of the Edinburgh surgeon and the small, tubby son of the Manchester textile merchant, to their misfortune, proved to have little sense of balance when practising turns on the barrack square and were mercilessly victimised by the sergeant instructor. I recall an occasion when the troop was practising about-turns on the slow march and my two pals simply could not keep their balance on the turn. The sergeant finally had them out in front of the troop while he expertly demonstrated and they patently failed to follow his example. He finally kept them with one leg suspended in the air until they collapsed, and he dismissed them with the disgusted comment: "You remind me of two dogs learning how to use a lamppost"! To the amazement of the troop the small, tubby man was the first to be awarded the single stripe of an acting, unpaid lance corporal because, when the troop later began practical training on tanks, the innate intelligence of my little friend made it easy for him to outshine everyone by his ability to grasp the mechanical principles and applications of tank drives, tank engines and tank guns.

About six weeks after I began military training I received a letter from Dr. Vernon, Head of the Psychology Department at Glasgow University, informing me that he had taken the trouble to summarise my thesis and have the summary published in the British Journal of Educational Psychology, where it had apparently attracted some favourable comment. His main purpose in writing was to enquire whether I could be granted leave of absence from military training to come to Glasgow and give a short address on my thesis to a seminar which he had organised. On receipt of the letter I made a blunder; for instead of taking it direct to the regimental office with a formal request for leave of absence, I took it to my sergeant instructor and asked his opinion of my prospect of securing leave of absence for two days. His reply was prompt and brutal: "Trooper Young, if you take that letter to the regimental office and ask for leave of absence, I shall walk in behind you and catch you when you are bloody well thrown out!"

At that point I knew that I dare not ask for leave of absence because, if I did, I would be in the sergeant's black book for the rest of my period at Catterick, which would have made my life an unbearable misery. That little episode marked a watershed, when I gave up all pretensions of ever pursuing an academic career and resigned myself to giving of my best in one of the humblest forms of human life: a recruit under instruction, requiring the minimum of intelligence but unquestioning obedience to instructions and orders however pointless and stupid they might be. I therefore replied to the letter from Dr Vernon, expressing regret that I was not allowed leave of absence from military training and thanking him for all the consideration and kindness that I had received from him.

Towards the end of my recruit training I was informed that I had been marked for transfer to an officer training unit whenever a vacancy occurred. In the meantime I had formed a friendship with a young schoolmaster from Lancashire who was such an enthusiast for motor cycling that he had applied and been accepted for training as a despatch rider. He was kind enough to make a request on my behalf to the officer in charge of despatch riders that I be allowed the use of a motor cycle to ride at the tail-end of the despatch riders in training, during the period when I was awaiting transfer to an officer training unit. To my surprise permission was granted, and I spent several weeks riding a 500cc motor cycle behind the trainee despatch riders. Furthermore my friend received permission to take me out alone during weekends to give me some cross-country training on a motor cycle, some of which was a little more than exhilarating, as it included ascent and descent of some of the steepest slopes of the Yorkshire dales. As a result of this intensive practice on a motor cycle, I was sometimes assigned the duties of despatch rider during my later period of training at OCTU.

In the late spring of 1941, after enduring an inclement winter at Catterick, I was transferred to Blackdown, near Aldershot, as an officer cadet in an armoured unit. There the standard of training on the barrack square, the standard of dress and deportment and the standard of barrack-room maintenance required of the cadets was even more rigorous than the corresponding standards at Catterick. In my opinion some of the spit and polish was quite bluntly and frankly ridiculous and, having regard to the requirements of a modern army in the field, was generations out-of-date. On the other hand most of the practical training on tanks and tank gunnery, especially the practical instruction given by experienced NCO's, was excellent and essential for the efficient conduct of an officer's duties in the field. The knowledge and practical skills of these experienced soldiers gained much more of my admiration and respect than did the blatant showmanship of some of the officer instructors, one of whose main purposes seemed to be to humiliate the cadets over the most minor lapses in spit and polish. I can still recall with loathing an incident where one of our most efficient cadets was put on a charge because the inspecting officer was determined to find some fault in the guard unit, and decided that the insteps of his boots between sole and heel were not sufficiently polished.

The cadets in our class were an interesting sample of the young men from various parts of the country and from various backgrounds who had been selected as potential officer material and, following my recent studies in Psychology, I found it absorbing to estimate their qualities. They represented a wide variety of family background, education, training, experience in employment and still more of character, personality and temperament. As we were perforce a closely-knit group in most of our training activities and in the large barrack rooms in which we slept, the characteristics and qualities of each cadet soon became obvious to all the others in the group. Before long I felt able to recognise a few who seemed to me to have the genuine qualities of leadership and who, in my judgment, if fortunate to survive the high rate of mortality among junior officers in armoured regiments, would inevitably secure rapid promotion on their merits. Another few might well gain promotion, not on their genuine qualities as leaders, but on account of their self-assurance or what in the Scottish phrase would be called "A guid conceit of themselves". Later experience confirmed my impression that one of the weaknesses of the army in wartime was a tendency to accept people on their own estimate of themselves, and that one of the most valuable properties was a plausible kind of "brass neck". Modesty was not a quality that was highly prized in the army.

As the only cadet in the class who had been brought up and wholly educated in Scotland, I was immediately marked by my Scottish speech and Argyllshire accent which I have retained throughout life. My fellow cadets quickly accepted me for what I was, but for some of the officer instructors my speech was obviously a minus mark. With some of the bright young cadets who had recently completed a degree course at university in England I was able to form quite a warm friendship, for they appreciated my greater maturity and the extent of my studies at university. In course of my training at OCTU the only activity at which I earned any credit was practical gunnery on the tank-training range which we visited in South Wales. There I was complimented by the sergeant major in charge because, according to his report, I was the only cadet who had been able to spot and guide my gunner on to every target on the range. There are occasional advantages derived from a rural upbringing.

As each class approached the end of their course at OCTU senior officers from regiments which had vacancies or pending vacancies for junior officers arrived to interview trainees. The only interview which I had was with the Colonel of the Second Lothians and Border Yeomanry, who was seeking officers of Scottish extraction and was prepared to accept me, provided that I passed out successfully from Blackdown and received my commission as an officer. The Lothians and Border Yeomanry was traditionally a cavalry regiment which drew its recruits mainly from the South of Scotland lying between Edinburgh and the Borders. In order to distinguish itself from the First Lothians and Border Yeomanry, the Second Lothians and Border Yeomanry preferred to be known as the Lothians and Border Horse, a title which was retained even when the regiment was equipped with tanks and became one of the three tank regiments in the Sixth Armoured Division, whose emblem was a mailed fist. The other tank regiments in the Division had also been traditional cavalry regiments: the Sixteenth/Fifth Lancers and the Seventeenth/Twentyfirst Lancers. When I joined the Division the Lothians and Border Horse was equipped with heavy Valentine tanks, driven by a diesel engine and armed with a two-pounder gun, while the other two regiments were equipped with more lightly- armoured cruiser tanks, driven by a petrol engine and armed with a six-pounder gun. While protected by heavier armour the Valentine tanks were much slower and less manoeuvrable than the cruiser tanks.

The uniform badge of the Lothians and Border Yeomanry was a wheat-sheaf which, on the officers' uniform, was not metal but a raised fabric finished in heavy gold thread. The jacket had epaulettes covered in blue and the peaked cap had a blue band. The jacket was traditionally worn with the top button undone. Among the junior officers it was a standing joke that we should not loiter in the door of a cinema or club in case we were mistaken for a commissionaire.

When I joined the regiment at the beginning of December, 1941, I was the junior second lieutenant in B Squadron which was detached and billeted in Nissen huts on an estate outside Cambridge. Most of that first winter was spent in the tank-park supervising the men on tank maintenance, however inclement the weather. As this entailed long periods of inactivity and insufficient exercise to stimulate the circulation, I found it thoroughly boring, At night I frequently acted as orderly officer in place of the young officers who wished to enjoy in Cambridge the kind of social activities which I had no desire to share. The squadron was commanded by Major Gordon Simpson, a young officer of outstanding ability and energy who later had the opportunity to prove his leadership in action and commanded the regiment with great distinction.

Some of my treasured memories of that period relate to Frank, the senior lieutenant, a very experienced regular soldier who had been promoted from the rank of regimental sergeant major in the Fifth Royal Lancers, a distinguished cavalry regiment. Frank presented the perfect image of a regular soldier, lean and hard with a lined but handsome face, an impeccable carriage and military bearing and a voice of command which one would expect from a former RSM of a cavalry regiment. When Frank took the morning parade of the squadron, which he frequently did, with the junior officers lined up behind him, he gave a perfect exhibition of how men should be commanded on parade and his control was immaculate. It was a splendid example to NCO's and junior officers.

As Frank was content to spend most of his evenings in the officers' mess, he and I shared many hours together when I was acting as orderly officer and I enjoyed his tales of life in the regular army. My only misgiving about these evenings was that Frank liked to drink beer which never seemed to affect his trim figure, while I as a keen long-distance runner had never become a beer drinker and had kept my alcohol intake to a minimum. Furthermore one of the less agreeable symptoms of my hair-trigger nervous system was a need to visit the lavatory after consuming several pints of beer. In Frank's company I felt that I had to keep my end up by matching his consumption pint for pint, with the result that I woke up in the middle of the night with an urgent need to relieve myself, and the nearest lavatory was some thirty yards from the hut in which I slept. To cover that thirty yards and back in the middle of a frosty night on snow-covered ground was more than adequate penance for the indulgence of the previous evening.

One of the troopers in our squadron was a young man with the dark-avised features of a gypsy, who was steeped in the lore of the countryside and would have been the ideal man to have on a survival expedition. Although I had been brought up on a farm in the Scottish countryside and had often used a catapult I would not have believed, unless I had actually seen, the amazing accuracy with which Darkie, as he was generally known, used a catapult. He could knock the head off a barn -yard fowl at ten yards. In the trees of the estate in which our squadron was billeted the pheasants regularly roosted, and it was widely known among the troops that Darkie could and did shoot the roosting pheasants from the trees with his catapult.

On the Christmas after I joined the regiment Frank, by virtue of his seniority and long experience, succeeded in getting leave to spend Christmas with his family. Having conceived the bright idea that it would be an unexpected and welcome gift for his family, he had a quiet word with Darkie about the prospect of getting a brace of pheasants to take home on his Christmas leave. Apparently Darkie promised to see what he could do. On the morning on which he was due to go on leave Frank was on his best form and insisted on taking morning parade. With his uniform pressed, leather polished, brasses shining, his cane tucked under his arm and the junior officers ranged behind him, Frank was confident and immaculate as he prepared to put the squadron through its paces. The men were all lined up when a small figure darted out of the nearest hut and took up position in the rear rank. Without identifying the culprit Frank rapped out an order: "Will that man who was late report to me after parade". When finally Frank gave the order for dismissal the small figure emerged from the ranks, marched smartly up to Frank, came to attention and said "Your pheasants, Sir", as he handed over a brace of pheasants. That was the only occasion in my experience when I saw Frank taken aback.

Towards the summer of 1942 various units of the Sixth Armoured Division were moved to Scotland, where the Lothians and Border Horse was billeted for a period under canvas and later in disused textile mills between Newmilns and Galston in Ayrshire. While stationed there we undertook a number of training exercises, including a combined landing with a commando unit at Castle Toward, Argyll; an extensive exercise with infantry which ended in Galloway and a rather disastrous exercise in North Ayrshire on moorland with boggy stretches in which some of our tanks threatened to sink out of sight.

On the combined exercise with the commando unit I blotted my record by missing the last transport in the evening to the ship on which we were billeted and having to spend the night at Castle Toward. When I boarded the ship on the following morning I narrowly escaped being put on a charge for absence without leave. On the extensive exercise in South West Scotland I was assigned to the duties of umpire and was paired with a major from the Polish troops in Scotland. He was a handsome, buccaneering character who claimed to be a member of a noble family in Poland and, judging from the conversation which I had with him, he was a Don Juan who was very attracted to Scottish women, especially young, married women. He told me that he had an ambition to leave many women pregnant, because he believed that he was doing Scotland a service by creating as many children as he could to carry on his noble blood line. By the time I met him he reckoned that he had more than a dozen illegitimate children and it was his firm intention to continue with the good work while he was stationed in Scotland. He was a man of considerable charisma who may or may not have been romancing, but on the exercise he was an amusing and interesting companion.

The exercise on the Ayrshire moors began badly and ended badly. For the journey to the exercise area the tanks were loaded on to transporters which took up most of the width of the narrower roads. A period of persistent rain had left the roadside verges and the moorland much softer than would normally be expected in the summer season. On a downhill stretch of a narrow road I saw the transporter immediately in front leave the road and plough into the soft verge, thus causing the heavy tank to burst its moorings and roll over the driver's cab crushing the driver and one of our best corporals who was seated beside him. When I reached the transporter the front had sunk so deeply and the cab was so flattened that I had to crawl in to examine the driver who had been crushed against the large steering wheel and was obviously beyond all aid. When I went round to the near side I was greatly relieved to find that the corporal was still alive and conscious, although he was lying crushed between the backrest and the seat, tightly wedged and unable to move. By this time a major from another squadron had arrived on the scene to take command.

When it became obvious that we could not move the corporal the major decided that the best course was to pull the tank, which was already inclined towards the near side, off the transporter and thus relieve the weight pressing on the cab. Another tank was driven into the adjoining field alongside the transporter, tow ropes were attached to the tank and the towing tank began to move away from the transporter. I had grave doubts about the effect of this manoeuvre on the cab of the transporter and on the corporal lying wedged underneath, but in the face of a decision by the senior officer I kept silent. As the towing tank moved away I knelt where I could keep a close watch on the corporal, and when the pressure was exerted on the nearside track of the tank bearing down on the cab I saw his face contorted and he moaned with pain. I immediately jumped to my feet and shouted an order to the NCO in charge of the towing tank to halt all movement which he did. The major glared at me and snapped an order to the towing tank to resume movement. At that point I must have completely lost control of myself, for I uttered a volley of oaths and yelled at the major that if he wished to kill the corporal he was going the right way about it. Impressed by that kind of abuse from a junior officer he halted the operation, and I then invited him to come and assess the situation for himself. Having done so he agreed with me that the tank could not be moved without grave risk to the corporal's life. By using every sharp tool we could find to destroy the backrest and seat we slowly and laboriously dug the corporal out and finally managed to free him, with a fractured pelvis and probably other injuries but alive. As he was sent to hospital and did not rejoin the regiment before we were sent overseas I had no opportunity to see him again, but I hope he recovered, for I like to think that I did something on that day to save the life of one of the finest young men in the regiment.

When our tanks reached the moorland area that had been selected and began to exercise, it was found that while some parts of the moor were firm other parts were so soft and boggy as to be quite unsuitable for the movement of heavy tanks. Later in the day when I was ordered to drive my three tanks through a soft area to reach a stated objective, two of the tanks got bogged down in a particularly wet area. From my years of experience as a youth on similar ground I selected a path which seemed rather firmer, but at one point the tank tracks began to churn the earth and I immediately ordered my driver to halt before the tank had sunk more than a few inches. My movement was observed by another senior officer who summoned me over and gave me a dressing down for risking my tank on ground where two others were already bogged down. I returned to my tank, instructed the driver precisely how I wished him to handle the controls, and very gently and slowly we emerged from the boggy patch on to firmer ground. From there I was able to tow the other two tanks out of the bog and we proceeded to our objective.

Late in the afternoon when I was taking my tank back to barracks without the aid of a transporter, I observed two of our tanks so deeply bogged down that one of them had the top of its turret almost at ground level. The final snag of the day occurred on the way back to barracks. When my tank met another vehicle on a narrow road my driver pulled over until one track was running wholly on the verge and the tank began to sink in the soft earth. Again I halted, got down in front of the driver and had him slowly reverse the tank on to the road. By this time in a vile temper with the events of the day, I quite unfairly gave my driver a dressing down and ordered him on no account to leave the hard surface of the road even if it forced some other vehicle off the road. Only when I was climbing back into my turret did I observe that a staff car filled with senior officers had drawn up behind my tank where they had no doubt heard me shouting at my driver. In the firm belief that my standing with the senior officers was already at rock bottom, I ignored the staff car and gave it no opportunity to overtake my tank until we reached the main road.

Later in the evening when I was dressing for dinner in the mess I saw my face in a mirror and was surprised at the blotches of dried blood which must have dripped on to me when I crawled into the cab of the transporter to get a good look at the face of the driver who had been bleeding from nose and mouth. I was sickened by the events of the day. In the mess after dinner I made a point of conversing with another junior officer while standing close by the major who had given me a dressing down earlier in the day, and in a very audible voice expressed the firm opinion that the senior officers who were responsible for the choice of the ground on which we had carried out that day's exercise deserved to be severely censured. I added that my opinion was based on over twenty five years of experience of similar countryside, climate and land conditions in Argyllshire, and that I was probably better equipped to judge these conditions than any other officer in the Division. As I had convinced myself that my future in the regiment was bleak, it came as a great surprise and comfort to me when my experienced friend Frank, who gathered opinions from the troops as well as the officers, joined me over a drink and said quietly: "Word has got around the regiment that you did well today".

One of the unexpected pleasures of being stationed in Ayrshire was that I was able to enjoy my first few months of domestic life with my wife. I first met the young lady who was later to become my wife in the mid nineteen thirties when I was still a student. At one of those dances which students organised in the thirties, when the evening began with the girls ranged along one side of the hall and the young men on the opposite side, as I looked across the room one girl seemed to me to stand out from all the others both in beauty and in sparkling vitality. Normally shy though I was, I was so eager to meet this girl and if possible get to know her that I rushed across the room when the first dance was announced to claim her as my partner. From that evening onwards we kept in touch and our relationship deepened until, a few years later, we went on a cycling holiday together to the North-West of Scotland. Somewhere on that holiday I plucked up sufficient courage to ask her if she would marry me and she consented. But I had been a poverty-stricken student and was now a poverty-stricken teacher, having part of my meagre salary deducted on account of part-time study. As my fiancee was also a teacher whose appointment would be automatically terminated on the date of her marriage, there was no possibility of retaining two salaries after marriage. Some period of waiting seemed inevitable.

In 1939 we were separated by the evacuation from Glasgow. My fiancee was sent with her pupils to a rural part of Aberdeenshire while I was sent to a rural part of Perthshire. When I returned to Glasgow my fiancee was retained in Aberdeenshire and I was fully occupied with teaching and study, including classes from 10am till 1pm on Saturdays. In 1940 I was called up for military service and later was transferred direct from Catterick to Blackdown.

During my period of training at Blackdown my fiancee was able to spend a few days in the vicinity of the OCTU in course of her summer vacation. That visit gave us an opportunity to have a full discussion about our future in the light of the virtual certainty that I would be sent on overseas service to face the possibility of death or serious disability. The main question at issue was should we get married as soon as possible or postpone it until the end of the war which might last for years. The lady made the decision as firmly and bravely as she has made many hard decisions in course of our married life. "If the worst comes to the worst", she said, "I should much prefer to be left a young widow than a girl who has just been left." "Splendid", I said, "Let's get married."

As I still had several months to spend at Blackdown completing my cadet training, we decided that the date of our wedding would be the day after I returned home on leave. In Edinburgh I collected my uniform from one of the two firms which made and supplied uniforms for officers in the Lothians and Border Horse, then took the train to Glasgow and on the following day turned up for my wedding ceremony and reception, having played no part in the previous preparations. Having attended only one wedding reception many years previously, I went through the ceremony blissfully unaware that I was required to make a speech at the reception. In the event the speech was pathetic but the guests readily forgave me.

During the reception some of the young men secured access to my luggage and stuffed shoes, socks, shirtsleeves and even the fingers of gloves with confetti. Because of my short period of leave and the problems of travel in the blackout, we did not go beyond Edinburgh for our brief honeymoon. On arriving at our hotel one of our first tasks was to spread a waterproof on the floor, clear all the confetti out of my clothing, bundle up the waterproof and wander along the streets in the blackout till we found an underpass on to which we tipped the confetti.

At the end of our honeymoon we boarded the train for Glasgow and found a first-class compartment which we thought we would have to ourselves until, within two minutes of departure, an elderly gentleman with briefcase and umbrella entered. From that point we tried to act like a mature married couple. As we approached Queen Street Station I lifted our luggage from the rack and when I pulled down my military greatcoat something like a cupful of confetti fell out of the deep revers of the sleeves and showered the compartment. The hearty laughter of the elderly gentleman filled the compartment before he wished us every happiness and made plain that he had not been in the least deceived by our attempt to behave like a long-married couple. On the following day I set out to join my regiment.

While the regiment was stationed in Ayrshire my wife managed to secure accommodation in a house belonging to the factor of an estate near Newmilns, and I was able to join her during my off-duty time by securing permission to live out. That arrangement gave my wife and me a short but happy taste of domestic life, and during a few days of summer leave we were able to visit Kintyre to see my family. The most important outcome of that period together was that before the Sixth Armoured Division embarked in the late autumn for overseas service, my wife knew that she was due to have a baby before the end of March, 1943 .

Chapter 12
Overseas Service

TOWARDS THE END OF November, 1942 the Sixth Armoured Division moved from North Ayrshire and embarked at Greenock, bound for the Mediterranean. I recall that my wife and I celebrated our first wedding anniversary and, before six o'clock on the following morning, I left my billet to join my regiment on the move. My wife has often recalled the memory of standing at the garden gate, listening to my footsteps fading into the darkness of the cold morning, and wondering whether she would ever see me again. For a young wife expecting her first child it was not a happy experience.

Our tanks, other vehicles and their crews were loaded aboard cargo vessels, while the rest of us travelled on passenger ships. Although the senior officers had probably been informed of our ultimate destination, the men and junior officers had no precise knowledge of either the theatre of war to which we had been posted or the port at which we should land. Fortunately for me, because of my extreme sensitivity to travel sickness, the voyage was relatively calm and, as far as I was aware, free from interference from submarines. Some of our troops who followed us in a later convoy were not so fortunate as the roll of honour of the regiment includes the names of a number of men who were lost at sea.

In the event we disembarked at Bone in Tunisia and moved into a prepared encampment to await the arrival of our tanks and other vehicles, with the crews which had accompanied them. As it happened the ships which carried the tanks also carried a mixed cargo, including supplies of gin and whisky. I can only conclude that the tank crews must have formed a happy relationship with the ships' crews, for cases of gin and whisky and generous supplies of chocolate had found their way into the turrets of most of the tanks, which landed with the crew commanders standing high in the turrets on cases of alcohol. Although the three tanks in my troop were among the minority which came off the ships with only some chocolate aboard, the quantity of alcohol floating around the camp was such that my troop ended the day with two four-gallon water cans, one more than half-filled with gin and the other with a similar quantity of whisky.

On that night I recall that I was Orderly Officer and for that reason had to remain relatively sober. Late at night I got properly dressed, tucked my cane under my arm, and walked through the camp to the guard tent on the outskirts. When I called the guard the only man to emerge was the guard commander who saluted and then steadied himself by holding on to a guy rope. As I could picture the condition of the men inside the tent, I refrained from ordering the corporal to turn out the guard and contented myself with a friendly talk. The guard commander was a university graduate who had no ambition to gain a commission and was content with the modest rank he had attained. When in course of the conversation I quoted a line or two from a poem by Robert Burns, he told me how much he admired the work of Burns and finished by claiming that, when he was drunk enough, he was liable to recite Tam o' Shanter from beginning to end. I at once replied: "Corporal, I think you may just be drunk enough tonight; let's have a go!" Without further persuasion he began and, with the occasional prompt from me, he completed the recitation of Tam o' Shanter to our mutual satisfaction. I then wished the corporal a peaceful night and retired to bed.

After a few days our tanks were loaded on to transporters and we began the journey eastwards towards the front line which, in the north of Tunisia, was in the vicinity of Medjez-el-Bab where a brigade of Guards, other infantry and a few parachute troops were opposed to a growing force of German troops, supported by artillery and tanks. The German troops also had the support of Junker JU87 dive bombers, commonly known as Stukas, which were formidable in their attack when not opposed by other aircraft. Those troops who were subjected to it would never forget the screaming and deadly dive of the stukas.

An incident which occurred when the long train of tank

transporters was travelling eastwards has remained in my memory. The native Tunisians generally tended to keep their distance and avoid our troops, but on this occasion a group of about a dozen horsemen, in full native dress and mounted on beautiful Arab horses, moved off the highway and paused on a knoll to allow the huge noisy convoy of transporters to pass. By chance the transporters halted for a short break just as my tanks were approaching the horsemen, who studiously ignored the stares of the curious troops. During this rest period another group of horsemen, comparable in number and equally well equipped, approached from the other direction and paused close to the first group. The two leaders moved together, placing their horses nose to tail, exchanged ceremonial greetings, conversed for some time, parted with the same ceremony and then each group moved off still completely oblivious of the troops and their monstrous machinery crowding the highway. That minor incident seemed to me to point the contrast between an ancient but civilised mode of life and a display of technology which was really an expression of modern savagery.

During much of the journey up to the battle area we had to endure persistent heavy rain and a chilly atmosphere not unlike the worst of the Scottish climate in late autumn. For the first time each tank crew had to sleep under a sheet of canvas attached to the side of the tank with its lower edge pinned to the ground; conditions which seemed initially strange, especially to the officers, but were soon taken for granted. It was not the most comfortable billet when the ground was muddy and a cold air pervaded the night. When we arrived at our destination near a small settlement called Bou Arada, the chief enemy of the tanks was mud: deep, gluey mud which clogged the tank tracks and the mens' boots and dried to a consistency of dried brick. The conditions were depressing and far from suitable for tank warfare. We had arrived in the middle of the rainy season in North Africa.

During the week of Christmas, 1942, while my regiment was held in reserve, the cruiser tanks of the Lancers, in atrocious conditions of rain and mud, endeavoured to give support to the Coldstream and Grenadier Guards and a battalion of American troops in a bitter battle to capture a strategic hill to which the British had given the name 'Longstop Hill'. Although the hill was much more heavily defended by German Troops than the British

Commanding Officer had anticipated, it was captured by the Guards after a hard and bloody battle and handed over to the American battalion. Scarcely had the Guards returned to their billets than they were ordered to march back to Longstop Hill. It was reported that a counter-attack had been made by a large force of German troops, supported by armour and artillery, which threatened to overwhelm the Americans who had been left to hold the hill. By the time the Guards reached their objective the American battalion had been routed, the German troops were dug in on the hill and the Guards, because of previous heavy casualties did not have the strength to retake the position. It was a most disappointing and morale-sapping outcome to what had initially appeared to have been an important and hard-earned victory by the British infantry. The strategic importance of Longstop Hill was that it commanded the lower ground stretching almost all the way to Tunis, and that was adequate reason for the determination of the German Command to hold it at all costs.

After the failure of the Allied forces to hold Longstop Hill a period of comparative stalemate on the Northern part of the front lasted for the greater part of January, 1943. The more Southerly section of the front in Tunisia, extending through Tebessa to Thala, Sbiba and Kasserine was held by American armour and infantry under the command of General Fredendall. Those forces were probing eastwards towards the coastal towns of Sfax and Sousse. In the central section of the front were the Free French troops who remained loyal to the Allied cause but who comprised only a minority of the French armed forces in Algeria and Tunisia. The majority of French civilians and military personnel, whether of the army, the airforce or the navy had no great love for the Americans or the British and either opposed the Allied landings in North Africa or remained aloof from the battle.

During January and the first half of February the Lothians and Border Horse engaged in occasional skirmishes with German tanks which resulted in some, though fortunately, not heavy casualties. I recall the first occasion on which we were ordered to sally forward from our higher position to lower ground, ostensibly to support our infantry who were being threatened by the advance of German tanks. As we lumbered forward in our heavy Valentine tanks I felt quite elated by our role of protecting the infantry. On the instructions of the squadron Commander I placed my three tanks close behind a line of trenches in which the ground troops had sought protection. No sooner had we arrived than the German artillery opened up and some of the shells began to land uncomfortably close. In a lull of the firing a sergeant major climbed out of a trench and ran towards me. He hurriedly saluted and shouted up to me: "For Christ's sake, Sir, get these crates of yours out of here; they're attracting all the shit in creation!" Only later was I able to smile at the thought of Sir Galahad riding to the rescue and being so suddenly and neatly brought down to earth. Yet it was obvious that the tanks stood out to the German artillery spotter who had promptly brought the guns to bear on us. To me it was a salutary lesson not to overestimate the value of our tanks in protecting ground troops.

In the course of my short period of active service I cannot recall being scared while in action inside a tank even though, as a junior officer in charge of three tanks, I invariably kept head and shoulders above the level of the tank turret to ensure close control of the movement of the tanks on either side. I shall never forget, however, an occasion on which I was paralysed with fear. The occasion arose from a decision by the higher command that, while we were stationed in a forward position, the junior officers should take turns to stand guard and maintain an outlook on enemy positions throughout the daylight hours. The usual guard position was a rock-covered knoll just forward of the tank laager. It happened that while I was on outlook duty the Colonel appeared with all the available officers of the regiment to conduct a TEWT (tactical exercise without troops) from the knoll which dominated the forward countryside. The large group of officers moving on the prominent outcrop of rock must have attracted the attention of a spotter for the German artillery, which promptly opened fire and quickly found the range for concentrated shelling. The Colonel and his officers quickly departed from the scene, leaving the lone sentry to his fate. As discipline and pride demanded that I must stand my ground, I compromised by lying flat on my face between two rocks. The German artillery was remarkably accurate and for the next twenty minutes or so I lay motionless, while the ground all around me was cratered with shells which peppered the rocks with shrapnel and pieces of flying stone. I should think that barely a yard of ground remained undamaged except the narrow space between the two rocks in which I lay, almost stunned by the noise of exploding shells and the whine of flying shrapnel. When the firing finally stopped I lay for several minutes, by some miracle completely unscathed, but so drained with fear that I could not stand up. By good fortune the experience did not leave any permanent scar but did, for many a day, make me humbly thankful for the gift of life.

Early in February our best tank drivers were selected, along with some senior personnel, to return to the rear area for intensive training on Sherman tanks, which had recently been shipped from the USA and which were designed to replace the outmoded and outgunned Cruiser and Valentine tanks of the Sixth Armoured Division. In my experience there were few aspects of the war on land which were more short-sighted and more damaging to the morale of our troops than the false and stupid propaganda which we were fed in Britain about the supposed inferiority and poor quality of German armament, tanks and military equipment in general. Imagine the shock when our troops in Tunisia came up against German tanks, to discover that their design, armour and mobility were of a very high standard and that their 75mm, and still more, their 88mm high velocity guns were vastly superior to the guns on our British tanks. My experience of pitting the two-pounder gun on a Valentine tank against a German 75mm or 88mm gun was comparable to pitting an air-gun against a high-powered rifle. In order to have a realistic chance of piercing the armour of a German tank the Valentine tank had to get within a range of a few hundred yards, whereas a German tank, equipped with a 75mm or 88mm gun could pierce the Armour of a British tank at up to more than fifteen hundred yards. I can recall firing at a German tank at a distance where the tracer was visibly losing elevation, and moments later a shell from a German tank gouged a lump of metal from the turret of one of our tanks. If that shell had hit the turret squarely the crew would probably have been killed. The first piece of German equipment which we captured was a BMW motor cycle with sidecar which seemed to me to be of superior design and finish to any comparable vehicle then made in Britain.

In the event the first of the Sherman tanks were assigned to American rather than British armoured units, and the Sixth Armoured Division had the unenviable task of fighting a crucial battle with its outmoded Cruiser and Valentine tanks, and also lacking the skilled services of its best and most experienced tank drivers. Soon after the middle of February we received orders that the whole Division had to move South as a matter of urgency without waiting for the use of tank transporters. As a result of these orders the tanks travelled on their tracks by day and night, with only the shortest of rests, until we reached our destination on a bleak stretch of moorland to the South of Thala and to the North of Kasserine. The journey was so wearing on the tanks that a number had broken down on the unpaved roads, and I found that I was among a minority of junior officers who still had three tanks in his troop when we reached our final refuelling depot in darkness and in pouring rain. As my crew went off to fill up the tank with diesel fuel I did my best to shelter under the canvas sheet which would form our bivouac for the night.

After a wet and restless night we were up at dawn to inspect the countryside and try to ascertain precisely where we were. Despite my best endeavours with the only map available to me, the surrounding area was so featureless, apart from the dirt road on our right, that I passed the whole day with only an approximate idea of my location. In the distance we could see, arising out of the plain, the hills through which ran the Kasserine gap. As usual the junior officers had received no information from the senior officers about the reason for our hurried move from North to South, nor any briefing about the military situation or about our immediate objectives. Rumours had nevertheless spread among the troops that the Sixth Armoured Division had been sent to plug a gap in the South of the battle front mainly due to the rout of American armoured units and infantry under the command of General Fredendall by tanks and infantry under the command of the formidable Field Marshall Rommel. There was a further depressing story that C, Squadron of the Lothians and Border Horse, under the command of Major Beilby, had been sent South as the armoured unit of a group called "The Gore Force" to reconnoitre the Kasserine Gap, and try to ascertain the precise state of the American forces in that area. The final depressing rumour was to the effect that The Gore Force had met the full might of the German tanks under the command of Rommel, that all the Lothians tanks had been destroyed and that Major Beilby with most of his men had been killed.

Although I had practically lost count of the days and the

dates, I had the impression that the date was twenty-first February. In that confused and depressing atmosphere the men of my troop did their best to brew up and cook breakfast on our sand-filled stoves, fuelled with petrol, and to cheer themselves up with the usual badinage and morning smokes. The tanks were then made tidy and prepared for action, the ammunition checked, the two-pounder gun and the machine gun cleaned and oiled, and the radio put on alert to receive any commands which might come from the Squadron Leader through Rear Link. Later in the morning the Division was ordered to take up battle position, with the Lothians and Border Horse on the left side of the road facing South and the Lancers on the right side. Perhaps because I had a full troop of three tanks, I was ordered to take position on the right front of our regimental position, while my friend David Gairns had taken position on the left front. Having deployed my tanks in a hull-down position behind a ridge, my only duty for the next few hours was to keep wireless watch in continuous contact with Rear Link. We had no definite information about the composition of the enemy forces or about the probable course of events.

In early afternoon the first line of heavy German tanks appeared in the distance and moved very deliberately but unhurriedly towards our front line. About the same time I received a personal order through Rear Link to take my three tanks forward and tow to the rear a battery of six anti-tank guns which had been deployed on our front. This my troop did and then resumed its forward position while the heavy German tanks approached ever nearer. It was fascinating though intimidating to have such a good view of the long high-velocity guns projecting beyond the front of the tanks. Being in a good hull-down position I was determined to hold fire until the enemy tanks were close enough to give the two-pounder guns on our tanks a realistic chance of making a kill.

Just at that time I happened to observe far away on our left flank a column of vehicles heading northwards, and I reported this movement to our Rear Link. A few minutes later Rear Link came back on the radio to say that the Brigadier in command of our action was very interested in my report and would I please give the precise map reference of the vehicles I had reported. The request for an exact map reference embarrassed me because I had been unable to pinpoint our own position accurately, but I did my best to comply with the Brigadier's command. I suspect, though I

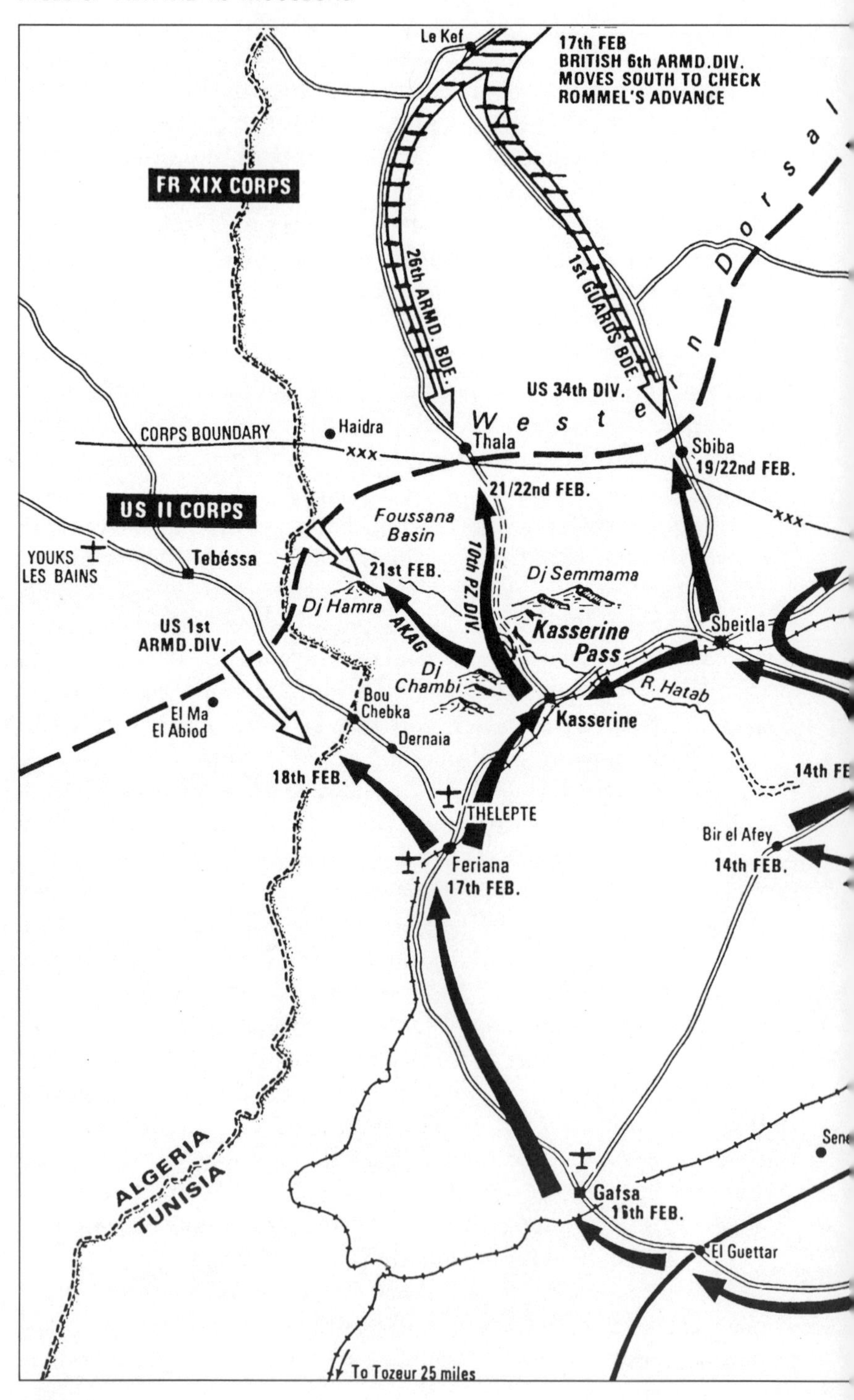

Le Kef
17th FEB
BRITISH 6th ARMD.DIV.
MOVES SOUTH TO CHECK
ROMMEL'S ADVANCE
FR XIX CORPS
26th ARMD. BDE.
1st GUARDS BDE.
Western Dorsal
US 34th DIV.
CORPS BOUNDARY
Haidra
Thala
Sbiba
19/22nd FEB.
21/22nd FEB.
US II CORPS
Foussana
Basin
YOUKS
LES BAINS
Tebéssa
21st FEB.
10th PZ. DIV.
Dj Semmama
Dj Hamra
AKAG
Kasserine
Pass
Sbeitla
US 1st
ARMD. DIV.
Dj
Chambi
R. Hatab
Bou
Chebka
El Ma
El Abiod
Kasserine
Dernaia
14th FE
18th FEB.
THELEPTE
Bir el Afey
14th FEB.
Feriana
17th FEB.
ALGERIA
TUNISIA
Gafsa
15th FEB.
El Guettar
To Tozeur 25 miles

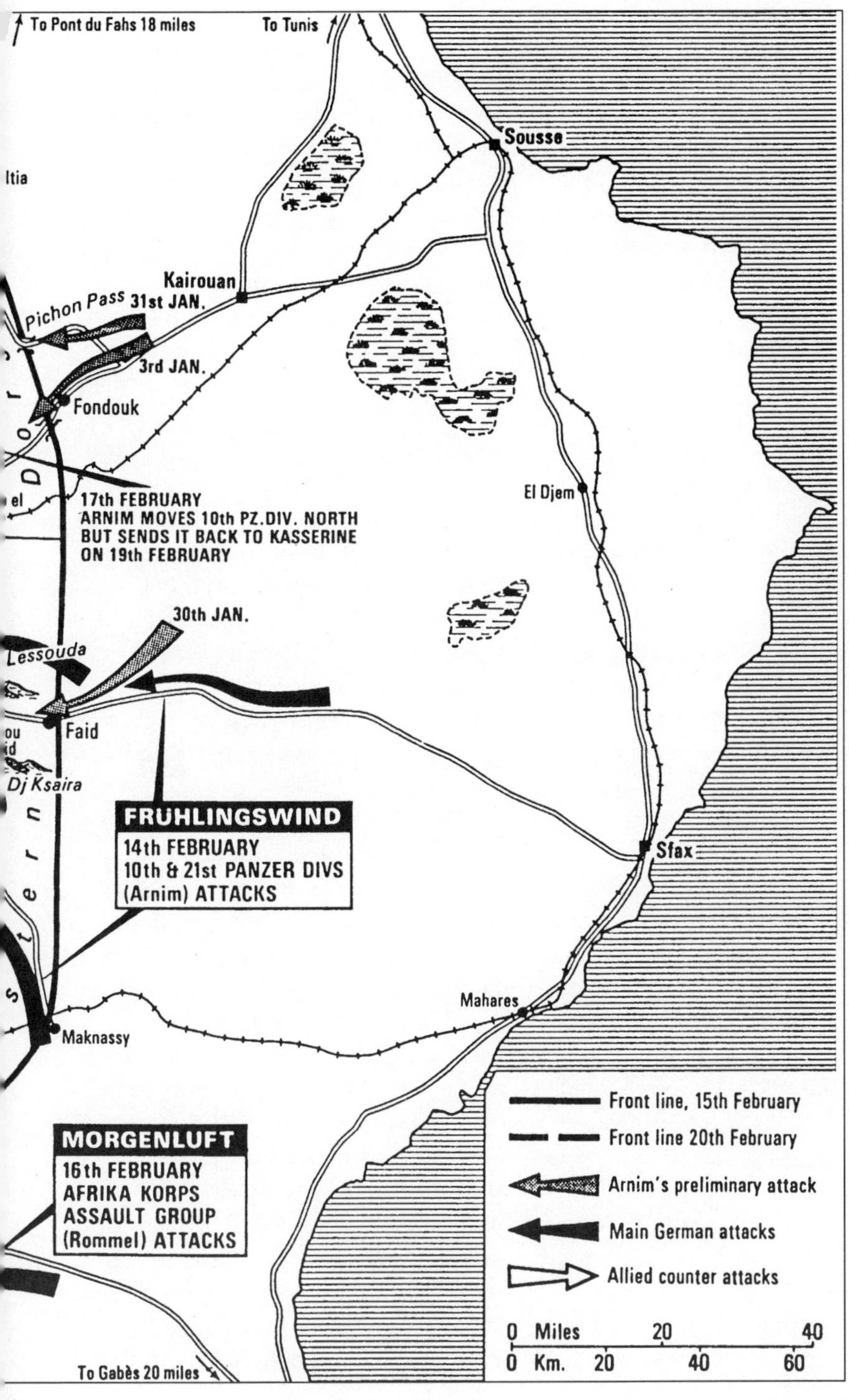
To Pont du Fahs 18 miles
To Tunis
Sousse
Itia
Kairouan
Pichon Pass
31st JAN.
3rd JAN.
Fondouk
El Djem
17th FEBRUARY
ARNIM MOVES 10th PZ.DIV. NORTH
BUT SENDS IT BACK TO KASSERINE
ON 19th FEBRUARY
30th JAN.
Lessouda
Faid
Dj Ksaira
FRUHLINGSWIND
14th FEBRUARY
10th & 21st PANZER DIVS
(Arnim) ATTACKS
Sfax
Mahares
Maknassy
MORGENLUFT
16th FEBRUARY
AFRIKA KORPS
ASSAULT GROUP
(Rommel) ATTACKS
Front line, 15th February
Front line 20th February
Arnim's preliminary attack
Main German attacks
Allied counter attacks
0 Miles 20 40
0 Km. 20 40 60
To Gabès 20 miles

do not know, that the information which I gave may have influenced the decision made by the Brigadier to order an immediate withdrawal of the Division, because of the danger that the Germans might be attempting an outflanking movement. The relatively slow and deliberate advance of the heavy tanks on our front might lead to the same conclusion.

As I had been eagerly looking forward to the chance of knocking out one or more German tanks from our well-chosen position, it came as a disappointment and a surprise to me when I received the order to withdraw. When my tanks had reversed and turned it became clear to me that the whole armoured brigade on both sides of the dirt road was in retreat. As we moved back from ridge to ridge the German tanks speeded up in pursuit and fire was exchanged from time to time. Suddenly I became aware that the engine of my tank was stuttering and failing to maintain normal power. After a short time it stalled and my driver failed to restart it. My corporal, Willie Grange, acted courageously and quickly by ordering his driver to return to my aid. My young gunner and I jumped down from our tank and attached a towrope from my corporal's tank to the front of mine, and his tank forged ahead until the engine of my tank again sprang to life. I then cast off the towrope and ordered my corporal to look after himself and his crew.

At that point I made a serious blunder which could have proved fatal, by deciding that my crew and I should not abandon our own tank. Although the engine had started under tow, it was obviously working at minimum power and could drive the tank only at walking pace. After a few minutes it again stalled. Since the German tanks were advancing steadily and all attempts to restart the engine failed, I ordered my crew to remove the breech block from both guns, grab their emergency rations and abandon the tank. Although shells were whining around, none of the crew was hit and we began to run. We ran until completely exhausted but had no hope of catching up with our retreating tanks and finally tumbled into a narrow, muddy wadi which was only a few feet deep. There we lay, unable to move, while the German tanks rolled past us and we began to hope that we could remain concealed until darkness fell. Our frail hopes were dashed by the German infantry who followed close behind the tanks in half-track vehicles. One of the tank commanders must have spotted us crouching in the wadi and reported our position by radio, for a half-track carrier deliberately ran along the side of the wadi until we were found, when a mounted machine gun was pointed at us and we heard the barked order which later became very familiar: "Raus!"

Much relieved at not being shot out of hand, we climbed out of the ditch and, greatly to our surprise, were hustled into the half-track from which we had the unusual experience of observing the rest of the battle from the side of the enemy. The mobility, comfort and roominess of the vehicle and the field of fire of the machine gun made a favourable impression on me. As none of my crew nor I could speak or understand German, communication was impossible until I tried my rudimentary French and found that one of the Germans could speak it fluently. Through him I learned how easily they had smashed through the American forces and how confident they were that their tanks were superior to the British tanks. These men were experienced troops whose morale appeared to be remarkably high and who were confident of victory.

After less than an hour of motoring the group of half-track carriers paused in front of a ridge on which was deployed a battalion of infantry who, as I learned later, were Leicestershires about to be engaged in their first major action. Most of the German tanks seemed to have passed through the Leicestershire position, although a few were attacking the infantry, mainly with machine guns. I later heard that the tank which led the attack was a captured British tank with which the Germans deceived the British troops. Dusk was now beginning to fall and in the rapidly fading light the half-tracks, with most of their troops still on board, speedily and efficiently winkled out some five hundred men of the Leicestershire battalion and lined them up on the dirt road to be marched southwards as prisoners of war. At that point my crew and I lost our comfortable ride in the German carrier and were bundled out to join the long column of prisoners. As the prisoners began to move off in the gathering darkness, some Leicestershire troops who had not been captured opened fire with a machine gun, obviously mistaking the moving column for Germans, and some of the prisoners were wounded. After a few minutes of confusion the wounded were removed, while the rest of us were rapidly marched away in the darkness. Only later did it occur to me that the short interval of confusion had presented a possible opportunity to escape into the growing darkness; an opportunity which never again presented itself. From then until May, 1945 I was securely held as a prisoner of war.

Chapter 13
Prisoner of War

FOR THE WHOLE NIGHT and part of the next day we marched southwards under guard until we arrived at some kind of German headquarters. Although there was a line of tents on one side of the road, these were reserved for the Germans and we were herded in the open air on the other side of the road. Fortunately the weather had improved and we lay exhausted, hungry and thirsty in relatively warm sunshine. This was the first opportunity my crew and I had to take stock of the situation, and I was surprised to find that I still had over my shoulder a small canvas satchel in which I had stuffed the heavy breech- block of our tank gun when we evacuated the tank and ran for our lives. While the breech-block had been buried in the mud of the wadi in which we had tried to hide ourselves, the bag still contained its usual contents which included shaving, washing and tooth-brushing materials, an emergency ration of chocolate, six rounds of ammunition for my. 38 revolver (the loss of even one of which would, in Britain, have landed me on a charge) and, finally, my black beret with the officer's badge of a wheat sheaf worked in raised gold thread.

Throughout the action of the previous day and the night march into captivity I had worn my steel helmet, without even realising that I was wearing it. When exhaustion and the warmth of the sun made me realise the stupidity of wearing the helmet, I discarded it and put on my black beret. The emergency ration of chocolate was shared with the crew but did little to satisfy our hunger and nothing to assuage our thirst.

My thoughts kept recurring to the puzzle of why our tank should have broken down at such an inopportune time when it had been running perfectly on the day previous to the battle and had done only a very short mileage on the day of the battle, I was also aware that it had been very carefully maintained by my loyal and hard-working crew. I was given the answer some twenty years later when I received a visit in Perthshire from Stan, the youngest member of my crew, who by then was engaged in running a cloth-factoring business but, at the time of our capture was barely twenty years old. While lounging in the garden on a warm summer day Stan and I recalled our wartime experiences, including the shock of being taken prisoner after the tank engine stalled, and he suddenly explained, for the first time, what he thought was the cause of the engine failure. On the night before the battle, in darkness and pouring rain, Darkie the tank driver, accompanied by Ken and Stan, drove to the fuel depot to refuel the tank with diesel oil. After they had poured in nearly thirty gallons of fuel, Darkie realised from the smell that something was wrong: that he had gone to the wrong fuel dump and had almost filled the tank with petrol designed for the engines of the Cruiser tanks. Although they did their best to get rid of the petrol and fill the tank with diesel oil, Stan was convinced from the engine failure on the following day that sufficient petrol had been left in the tank to cause the trouble. In order to protect Darkie they decided not to tell me of the mishap, as they hoped that no damage had been done. If they had told me of the occurrence I should probably have abandoned the tank more quickly when the engine stalled but, as I told Stan, we were fortunate that we all lived to tell the tale.

As we lounged on the ground I was taken by surprise when a German officer approached, seized me by the arm and led me to one of the larger tents which was occupied by a group of German officers, three of whom were seated behind a trestle table. The senior officer in the middle addressed me in fluent English. For the next fifteen minutes or so I was closely questioned and pressed very heavily to give information about my unit and my activities beyond the minimum of name, rank and number to which I obstinately adhered. When I had really begun to fear that I might be taken out and put before a firing squad, the senior officer finally paused and gave an order to a junior officer who departed from the tent. After an interval of tense silence the officer returned and placed before his senior a large, heavy book. The three officers at the table leafed through the book for some time, paused at one page and then the whole atmosphere relaxed. Turning to me with a smile the senior officer said courteously: "I regret, Lt. Young, that we felt it necessary to press you so hard, but from your cap badge we concluded you were from a parachute unit, and our intelligence people had no report of British parachute troops having been dropped in this area. We now realise that you are an officer in the Lothians and Border Yeomanry. You may now return to your companions. "It had not previously occurred to me that the raised wheatsheaf on my beret did resemble the image of an open parachute.

Later in the day there was an obvious stirring of excitement among the German troops which indicated that something unusual was expected. Suddenly a small convoy of vehicles arrived in the camp and from one of these emerged Field Marshall Rommel, who walked through part of the camp with his entourage. That was my one and only sight of the great man in person and at such a distance that I could decipher nothing of his facial expression, but he was obviously regarded with awe by his men. Only many years later did I read that by the time I had a glimpse of him he was a sick man, worn out by the long campaign in the inhospitable climate of North Africa and on the verge of being transferred back to Germany. Barely a year later, despite the sterling service which he performed in strengthening the coastal defences of France, he was in disgrace and close to death for suspected treason. "Sic transit gloria belli!"

Largely due to hunger, thirst and exhaustion, exacerbated by the natural depression which afflicted most prisoners of war when first captured, my memory of the next few days of travel is confused and uncertain. The first few weeks of captivity were particularly difficult for me because of my persistent worry about my wife. As my crew and I had been left behind by our retreating forces and were completely alone when taken prisoner, I was well aware that the first intimation which my wife received would be a telegram from the War Office reporting with regret that I was missing. I was also aware that she would receive that intimation within a week or two of the birth of her child, and I dreaded to think of the shock she would suffer and the effects it might have on her health and wellbeing at such a critical time. Only much later did I learn that by good fortune she was spared the immediate shock. Her brother, Norman, who was an officer in the Merchant

Navy, happened to be home on leave when my wife was advised to enter a nursing home in Glasgow prior to the birth of her child. Norman intercepted the telegram from the War Office which was delivered after his sister had gone to Glasgow and he wisely decided to withhold the information until the baby was born and my wife had returned home to Kilcreggan on the Firth of Clyde. By that time the International Red Cross had been able to report that I was a prisoner of war in Italy. When a letter finally reached me with the news that my wife and baby were safe and well in Kilcreggan, it felt like a burst of sunshine piercing the clouds, and I resolved to let nothing worry or depress me however long the period before I again saw my family.

My next clear recollection is of being herded into a barbed wire enclosure on the outskirts of a coastal town, which could have been either Sfax or Sousse. Within this POW cage there had been dug a series of small trenches about six to seven feet in length, about four feet in width and between two and three feet deep. These trenches provided the only meagre shelter from the chilly winds which blew at night. Fortunately the winter rains had ceased, the sunny days were quite warm and the floors of the trenches were dry and sandy. Throughout the journey towards the coast I had paid little attention to anyone other than my crew. As darkness fell on the POW enclosure I dropped into one of the shallow trenches and there was joined by a young lieutenant who informed me that he was a subaltern in the Royal Engineers and was known as Bob. It was much later before I learned that his given name was Ivan but in the services he had acquired the even shorter name of Bob, and Bob he was known to his fellows until our release from POW camp in May, 1945. He had been captured by the Germans when he was out in command of a small mine-laying unit and had penetrated too far beyond the Allied front line.

In return I told him that my name was Lachie (shortened from Lachlan) but that if he preferred to avoid the name he could call me by my initials: LB. I had learned from experience that many of my English friends found difficulty with the sound of 'ch' as in 'loch'; tended to pronounce my name as 'Lackey' and occasionally asked me when and where I had acquired such a demeaning byname. In order to establish the respectable provenance of my given name, I was wont to explain that the clan Lachlan had been based for many centuries in Argyllshire; that it was more commonly found in the form of a surname 'McLachlan', members of the family or clan of Lachlan; that there was still a Castle Lachlan on the eastern shore of Loch Fyne, and that the surrounding lands still belonged to the chief of clan Lachlan.

After conversing for some time in the growing darkness Bob and I lay down side by side in the same trench and slept quietly until sunrise. From that day until our release from POW camp we remained together as firm friends and partners, sharing the experiences and occasional hardships of prison life and giving each other material and moral support as far as we could. Although younger than I, Bob was already a highly-qualified civil engineer who hoped to specialise in soil mechanics, and he had the additional qualities of being artistic and skilled in handicraft; qualities in which I was notably lacking. I still possess as mementoes some of his sketches of a POW camp And a tin mug with handle which he fashioned for me and which I used throughout my period as a POW. It must be difficult for anyone who has not been through the experience to appreciate the value which prisoners placed on such apparently trivial articles.

The next stage of our journey was by train to Tunis, where we were crowded into still another enclosure which was attached to a disused tobacco factory. There we spent most of our time in the open air, with little room for exercise, fed mainly on slops which were cooked in large boilers and ladled into containers. As far as I can recall we slept on straw-filled palliasses on the floor of the factory, where we could also find shelter from rain. As we had been well fed (perhaps over-fed) on pack rations during our period of active service, the pangs of hunger grew on us with each passing day in POW camp.

By some chance which I cannot explain neither the German soldiers nor the Italians in whose custody we had been placed removed from me the small canvas shoulder-bag which I had retained in my possession throughout the tortuous journey from Thala southwards then eastwards to the coast and then northwards to Tunis. In the POW enclosure at Tunis I began to appreciate the full value of the contents of the satchel; for it contained a toothbrush and paste, a face-cloth and small towel, my black beret and, best of all, a safety razor with a packet of spare blades. I still possess as a memento the safety razor, which I used throughout my period in POW camps and which may actually have achieved a record in the number of faces it has shaved. In the enclosure at Tunis it appeared to be the only razor available and it was passed from one officer to an other until the blade became so blunted it would no longer cut. Even then attempts were made by some of my companions to hone the spent blades by rubbing upon a piece of fine sandstone and on a leather belt. If anyone succeeded in honing a blade he did not return it to me, but I am happy to say that the razor was invariably returned to me after it had gone the rounds. In our later sojourns in other camps the razor was frequently borrowed but always returned to my possession, which I regard as a tribute to the character of my fellow-prisoners.

Eventually we were moved aboard an Italian ship in Tunis harbour where we hoped, as it proved vainly, that we would be more adequately fed. On board ship the officers and other ranks were completely separated, when the men were crowded into the lower decks of the ship and kept behind bars. If in course of the subsequent journey to Italy the ship had been sunk, I am virtually certain that none of the men would have been released and that all would have perished, for the Italian crew seemed to live in a permanent state of alarm. After loading the ship moved out into the channel at Tunis, where a few of the officers who were fluent in Italian learned that, in addition to the prisoners of war, she also had on board a dozen Arab steeds which were being sent as a personal gift to Mussolini from an Arab sheik. For the better part of a week the ship lay idle in the channel because, we were led to understand, reports had been received of a British naval force patrolling the sea between Italy and Tunisia. Before departing for Italy, the ship returned to the harbour at Tunis in order to replenish the water supply which had been virtually exhausted, partly due to the quantity of water required for the Arab horses, evidently regarded as more important and precious than the prisoners held in the bowels of the ship.

During the period of about ten days on which we were aboard the ship the daily ration of food served to the officers consisted of a few ounces of tinned meat and one ship's biscuit, supplemented by water. As the officers were not allowed to visit the other ranks I cannot confirm whether or not they were given the same ration, but I learned later that in course of the voyage the soldiers had traded most of their personal belongings, such as rings, watches, and penknives for scraps of food thrust through the bars by members of the Italian crew. For at least some of the officers the inadequate ration was supplemented on one occasion by an invitation from the ship's captain to one officer to be his guest at a meal in the officers' quarters. I was fortunate to be one of the officers to receive the captain's invitation, although my enjoyment of a satisfying meal was rather dulled by my lack of fluency in Italian. Apart from that kindly gesture from the Italian officers, which was much appreciated, I have nothing but unhappy memories of the voyage, which was made the less relaxing by the permanent state of alarm of the crew, who moved about in their unlaced footwear obviously ready to abandon ship at any moment.

Without incident the ship arrived at the port of Naples, which caused one of my fellow-officers to remark: "We have all heard the phrase, 'See Naples and die'; but much more fitting for the atmosphere around here would be, 'Smell Naples and die!" After some delay, which included the unloading of the precious horses, we disembarked and were transported to a POW camp which we later learned was a transit camp outside Capua. There the officers were finally separated from the other ranks and were housed in huts in a compound which was far from pleasant. The food was so bad that most of us suffered from prolonged bouts of diarrhoea, or perhaps even dysentery, which made days and nights decidedly unpleasant. The lavatories, though foul, were not the worst I have experienced but they were among the busiest, as that was the only camp in which I can recall having had to queue for the use of a lavatory at three o'clock in the morning. In addition to discomfort boredom was endemic, because so many of those recently taken captive had not emerged from the initial stage of accidie and depression. Some were loath to get out of bed in the morning, and some were loath to care for their appearance by washing and shaving. Their morale had sunk to a low ebb.

A splendid example was set by a captain who was a regular soldier and who had been promoted to commissioned rank. Every morning he was out of bed before seven o'clock, brushed his boots and rubbed up his buttons, washed, shaved and went out for a smart walk in the compound before the usual tasteless breakfast. He illustrated to perfection the one feature of the regular army which I most respected: the installation of habits of discipline and pride in appearance even under the most adverse conditions. To most of my fellow-officers staying in bed in the morning was no treat, for the palliasses and the hessian sheets hooked to metal frames which supported them were infested with bedbugs. On sunny days the palliasses and supporting sheets were carried into the open air where the bedbugs were hunted and killed. As I did not suffer bites I always maintained that my bed did not harbour bugs. When after a time one of my companions insisted that my palliasse and sheet be taken outside for examination, I was shocked to find that my bed was heavily infested with bedbugs. It seemed that the bugs lived with me and sallied forth at night to feed on my companions. Whatever may be the cause, I discovered that I was one of those queer specimens who were immune to bedbugs. Later in life, when I regularly visited schools, I occasionally picked up on my clothing a flea which I presume sought the warmth of my skin. Almost invariably the first person to become aware of the flea was my wife when, lying in bed at night, she felt the first bite and immediately began an urgent search for the intruder. The same applies to the red spider mite (berrybug) which regularly afflicts my wife towards the end of summer but leaves me entirely unmolested. Sadly I can claim no immunity from the Scottish midge nor from the mosquito.

Because of the lack of books and reading material in the camp and the lack of recreational activities, I canvassed some of my fellow-officers about the possibility of organising a programme of talks on topics which might attract an audience and encourage a discussion. Those of us who were prepared to stand up and deliver a talk went around assiduously encouraging others to give even a 'my job' talk, until we had compiled a surprisingly varied programme which proceeded to our mutual satisfaction. About that time two young officers from the Brigade of Guards arrived in the camp. They gave the impression of being in their early twenties, tall and slim, looking more like students who had recently graduated from college than like officers who had endured battles and bloodshed like that at Longstop Hill in Tunisia. I regret that the name of one of these young officers has escaped my memory but the other was Lord Brabourne. When they had become familiar with the routine of the camp lord Brabourne, to my surprise because of his youth, volunteered to give one of the talks in our programme. My concern was needless. To the delight and surprise of his audience, Lord Brabourne gave a most interesting and informative talk on football: not rugby football; not the wall-game at a famous public school but good, old-fashioned traditional soccer. He referred to the history, organisation and development of football in England and reminded us of many of the outstanding games, incidents and personalities, especially of the nineteen thirties. He then surprised the audience even more by volunteering to act as 'memory man' by answering questions put to him on football games, prominent players and personalities during the previous ten years, and he fielded almost every question, Whatever else Lord Brabourne did or did not know, he quite obviously had acquired an almost encyclopaedic knowledge about football, with the result that his standing in the camp was transformed.

After some weeks we were transferred from the discomforts of the transit camp at Capua to a permanent camp at Modena in the North of Italy, where we were accommodated in well-built quarters which had, I believe, served as a barracks for the Italian army. The prisoners occupied a series of long barrack rooms, not unlike large hospital wards, with lavatory facilities at one end and at the other end a single room which was assigned to an officer of the rank of Lt. Colonel who acted as officer in command of the barrack room. This was by far the most comfortable building which we ever occupied as prisoners of war, although we had to become accustomed to squatting in place of sitting on a WC pedestal., During our stay of less than six months in Modena over the spring and summer of 1943 we had only minor complaints about physical treatment, since the Italian Commandant even arranged occasional walks for groups of prisoners in the countryside surrounding the camp, and our only complaint about the weather was the summer heat. Although the food supplied and cooked by the Italians was deficient in quantity and still more in quality, it was supplemented by the contents of food parcels which arrived at irregular intervals from the International Red Cross. On one occasion a supply of good quality raisins was received from South Africa, perhaps because of the large number of South African officers in the camp, and with these the Italian cooks made a very satisfying rice and raisin pudding which I certainly ate with relish, and which has remained one of my favourite puddings for the rest of my life. I also recall that we received with fair regularity a supply of wine (vino) which was poured into our mugs and which was so poor in quality that I could not enjoy it and usually gave my share to a fellow-officer who relished it. He was an officer from South Africa who occupied a bed near mine and kept beside the bed a mug of vino from which he took a drink first thing in the morning. As the stuff would almost burn a hole in a rug I could not but admire the strength of his stomach.

When the Italian Government in September 1943 decided to teminate hostilities, the Commandant of our camp apparently gave the Senior British Officer no prior warning, and only when our guards disappeared from the camp did most of us become aware of the collapse of the Italian forces. Although the camp was left unguarded for the better part of a day, the officers in the barrack blocks, strange as it may seem in retrospect, were ordered to remain within the camp compound. Since we were still under military discipline, with a senior officer in command of each barrack block, almost all of us obeyed orders and remained in position. I still have in my possession a postcard which I wrote on that day to my wife, but which was never posted, informing her that we had been liberated from POW camp and that I hoped to be home soon to see her and my baby son. Imagine our shock when, instead of being liberated, the camp was surrounded by German troops from an SS unit, who gave us the minimum of time to collect our belongings, marched us to the railway station, packed us into enclosed wagons which had originally been designed as horseboxes and sent us on our way to Germany.

As I almost invariably found in my day-to-day activities throughout my military service, the junior officers and other ranks received either no information or the minimum of information about the situation in which they found themselves or the action in which they were engaged. Almost fifty years after the event I still do not know with certainty why the officers in our camp at Modena were ordered to remain in an unguarded camp compound for the better part of twenty four hours after our Italian guards had fled. The tale which I heard later was to the effect that we had in our camp a group of over a dozen senior officers who were the immediate subordinates of the Senior British Officer, and who maintained order and discipline in the barrack blocks. Apparently this group of senior officers claimed to have received intelligence that the objective of the Allied forces, immediately following the Italian surrender, was to cut across the North of Italy and entrap the German forces in the peninsula. In accordance with this strategic plan, Senior British Officers in Italian POW camps had received instructions that the prisoners were to remain in the camps until they received further orders, and were on no account to disperse and wander over the countryside. Apparently the only officer in our camp who refused to conform was a South African colonel who collected the officers from his own battalion and walked out of the camp. I cannot confirm that the tale which I heard was accurate, although there must be some explanation for the orders which we received from our senior officers to remain inside a camp from which the Italian guards had fled.

Packed inside the horseboxes, which had apparently been used for the transport of coal and were filthy with coal dust, we travelled towards Germany in very hot, sunny weather. This added to the discomfort of the dirty, ill-ventilated and overcrowded boxes, with only one small, barred window through which a few of us at a time could look with longing at the clusters of grapes hanging on the vines close by the railway line. Although too depressed and discouraged to be much concerned about food, we suffered severely from dehydration and thirst. That journey, after the false euphoria of the previous day, I recall as one of the low points in my POW experience.

As the horse-boxes in which we travelled were old and poorly maintained, it transpired that some of our fellow-prisoners were able to make an opening through which to attempt an escape. The first small group who tried to escape were spotted by the German guards who succeeded in recapturing them, bound them hand and foot and bundled them into an open carriage to be baked by the sun. At the same time a warning was issued through the Senior British Officer that in the event of any further attempt at escape the prisoners concerned would be shot. Among the next group who attempted an escape were young Lord Brabourne and his companion. The train was again brought to a halt, the prisoners were pursued and apparently the commander of the German guards reported that they had been shot while trying to escape. As the information which I received about these attempted escapes was conveyed to me after our arrival in Germany, I am unable to confirm the accuracy of all the details.

Several years later I read in my morning newspaper a short article about the 'wedding of the year', the wedding of the daughter of the Earl Mountbatten to Lord Brabourne, at which it was anticipated the members of the Royal Family would be among the guests. My heart leaped as I asked myself if this could possibly be the Lord Brabourne whom I had briefly known in Italy, and if the German officer had been bluffing when he reported that the small group of prisoners trying to escape had been shot. At the first opportunity I consulted a volume on the peerage in the County library, only to reap disappointment by reading that the present Lord Brabourne had succeeded to the title following the death of his elder brother while on military service in Italy in September, 1943. The German SS officer had not been bluffing.

When our train finally arrived at its destination in Germany and we were unloaded in a bedraggled, filthy and weary condition from our containers, I was unable to find out the identity of the station or the location of the camp in which we were temporarily housed. Because of the extreme difficulty which prisoners found in acquiring possessions, including spare clothing and underwear, toilet necessities, cooking and eating utensils, tins for the cooking and storage of food, extra blankets, books, paper and writing materials, they had a compulsive tendency to hoard and treasure all their meagre goods, especially when they were transferred from camp to camp, with the result that on the move they were laden like mules. On the day of our arrival in Germany we had to walk quite a distance, in heavy rain, from the station to the prison camp, with our personal possessions hanging and clattering around us in makeshift bundles or tied on with string. When the prison gate opened, the long, ragged column of prisoners was hustled through on to a roadway with prison compounds on either side already well filled with prisoners. There we paused in utter exhaustion and dejection, still bitterly regretting the lost opportunity to escape from the unguarded camp in Italy and feeling doomed to spend the rest of the war in such enclosures as loomed on either side of us, Although most of the men in the compounds paid scant attention to us, a group of men in American airforce uniform were sufficiently interested to approach our heavily-burdened column and inspect our condition from the other side of the boundary fence. After some minutes of silence a very large American stretched his hands wide to grasp the wire and exclaimed: "My Gawd, and somebody told us you guys was mechanised!" That was the kind of tonic that was desperately needed and a ripple of laughter spread along the column of weary prisoners.

That first camp in Germany proved to be merely a staging

post, as we were almost immediately transported westwards towards the border with France, where we were crowded into an old fort which had apparently been built and occupied by German forces at the time of the Franco-Prussian War of 1870. The fort was built wholly underground, three floors in depth, with grass and shrubs on the surface and entered by a winding roadway which descended into the depths. At the first and second level, into which some twelve hundred prisoners were crowded, there was an almost continuous space bounded by the outside walls and almost bare of furnishing. Along large sections of the exterior walls long wooden platforms had been constructed to serve as sleeping quarters, and these were strewn at intervals with straw-filled palliasses and rough, grey blankets. In order to share the available bedding and blankets the prisoners huddled together on the platforms like pigs in a pigsty.

The lavatories were formed of a continuous wooden structure about two feet in height, covered by wooden planks with holes at intervals. The excrement fell to a sump under the fort causing a continuous smell to which we had to become accustomed. That continuous malodorous atmosphere was as nothing compared with the almost overpowering smell which occurred at intervals when the sump was cleaned out by some kind of suction apparatus, and the waste loaded into tankers for disposal. By day and night we had to live by artificial light, with no opportunity for exercise outside and no leisure amenities inside the fort. About the food supply and how it was cooked and served I have no recollection.

The most depressing aspect of the initial period of POW life in Germany was the conviction which spread among the prisoners that this was the normal standard of provision for war prisoners in Germany, and that we might be immured in this dungeon for the duration of hostilities. The very thought was enough to make people feel suicidal. Fortunately these primitive conditions had to be endured for only a few weeks, when we were moved eastwards to a permanent camp near a pretty village called Weinsberg, which was situated in attractive rolling countryside to the East of Heilbronn and north of Stuttgart and was known as Oflag 5 (a) . We were informed that it had originally been built to serve as a Hitler Yugend Camp.

The prison compound was about 400 metres long by 100 metres wide, surrounded by a strong double fence over 10 feet high, with tangled rolls of barbed wire between the fences. At intervals around the perimeter were tall covered watchtowers, with armed guards, search lights and telephones to the guard house. A single tripwire which the prisoners were forbidden to cross ran round the compound a few yards from the inner fence. Within this enclosure were two rows of timber huts, mainly single storey, of which nine formed the prisoners' living accommodation, while the rest comprised administrative, communal, dining and kitchen accommodation. The residential huts were divided up into ten living rooms, each about 24 by 20 feet, with a central passageway and communal lavatory accommodation at one end. Depending on the total number of prisoners in the camp at any time, each living room was furnished for fourteen or sixteen prisoners, with seven or eight double- tiered bunks leaving just enough room to move between them, one or two high cupboards, a locker between each two prisoners, a central table and some stools. Heating in winter was provided by a freestanding stove with a smoke-pipe leading into a vent in the wall next to the passageway. The windows were heavily barred. In each room lived, played, argued read and slept a group of fourteen or sixteen men who, in winter, were confined to their hut from sunset till morning roll-call.

The additional accommodation included a hut for camp administration, a kitchen and communal dining and recreation room, medical clinic and hospital premises and a hut used for educational, examination and library purposes. The internal administration of the camp was organised by the Senior British Officer, who in Oflag 5a was a South African officer, his adjutant and administrative staff. As officer prisoners could not be employed inside or outside the camp by the German Authorities, we had in the camp about a hundred British other ranks who carried out cleaning, cooking and maintenance duties under the supervision of German guards. As time passed it was interesting to see the camaraderie which developed between the British and German troops, despite the language barrier. On one occasion when a hand-cart was in use to move cupboards, I was amused to see a stout German guard help to push the laden hand-cart while a smaller British soldier carried the guard's rifle.

The layout of the camp lent itself to the assignment of residential huts to national groups, including about 100 from Australia, 150 from New Zealand, 300 from South Africa, 500 from

Britain and a few from Canada. One hut was occupied by the men who were largely responsible for the manual work around the camp. When the camp became fully operational the aspects which struck me most forcibly were the efficiency of its internal organisation and the richness and variety of its cultural, social and educational life. The efficiency is perhaps not surprising, because the military framework of organisation was still there, as was the military tradition of discipline which, granted good leadership, can function with speed and efficiency. A less obvious factor was the nature of the community: a compact group of adult men, almost all in the prime of life, the majority well above average both physically and mentally, many endowed with special abilities and talents, relieved of all domestic and family responsibilities, with no dependants young or old, relieved of all normal work and with ample time on their hands.

One of the largest and most efficient organisations in the camp was the escape department, better known as 'the cloak and dagger' department, under the control of the escape committee led by an officer of outstanding ability from South Africa, who proved his qualities of leadership in the post-war world when he turned to politics and became Leader of the Opposition in the South African parliament. The escape committee coordinated and closely supervised all attempts at escape, which were a continual preoccupation of a number of prisoners and must have engaged the energies of hundreds at some time during our occupation of the camp. As I was at no time closely concerned with the escape department my knowledge of the attempts to escape, which went on continuously, was gained at second-hand and may be far from accurate.

The energy and ingenuity devoted to projects for escape were unbounded, wholly admirable and kept many prisoners physically and mentally in first-class condition, even though the number of escape attempts which succeeded was pitifully small. During almost the whole period of our stay in the camp numbers of prisoners were engaged in the planning and digging of tunnels although, as far as I am aware, no one succeeded in escaping through a tunnel. Secret tunnelling presented many problems, among the greatest of which was the disposal of the spoil: the soil and debris excavated from the tunnel. The many reports of attempts at escape which I heard at second-hand included a tale about one of the last tunnels attempted in the camp. Previous tunnels had been dug in a direction which took them away from the buildings occupied by the Germans, and none had proved successful. Someone conceived the idea that a tunnel directed under the boundary fence towards the German administrative buildings might stand a better chance of success. The plan was therefore to dig a tunnel from the hut in our compound which was nearest to a hut in the German quarters normally used for the storage of Red Cross parcels, and to emerge under the floor of that hut. In order to speed up the rate of tunnelling a number of storage cupboards were emptied and the spoil was stored in the empty cupboards. Because of overcrowding of the camp, and in order to make room for extra two-tiered bunks, some cupboards had been moved from the rooms into the central passageway, and some of these cupboards had been used for the storage of spoil.

While the tunnel was being dug, the occupants of an adjoining room had reported that the stove in their room was spewing out smoke, probably due to an accumulation of soot in the wall-vent, and this report had been conveyed to the German administration. According to the story which was related to me, the tunnelling party made excellent progress and were confident that the tunnel had actually reached a point under the floor of the hut where the exit was to be made. By unhappy coincidence, on the day preceding the night on which the exit from the tunnel was to be made, a German guard arrived in the adjoining room with workmen who had been instructed to repair the defective stove. Having cleaned the interior of the stove-pipe which led into the wall vent, the workmen and guard then went into the central passage to remove from the wall a metal plate which gave access to the vent. In order to get access to the metal plate, they had to move one of the tall cupboards which had been removed from the room. The cupboard proved to be so heavy that a team of several men failed to budge it, and when the German guard insisted on opening the cupboard door he was deluged with spoil from the tunnel. It is easy to imagine the depression which might afflict a prisoner, or even a group of prisoners, who had devoted many weeks of mental and physical effort to the planning and digging of a tunnel, only to be frustrated by its accidental discovery when the project was on the verge of success.

Another escape project of which I was informed also related to storage cupboards. When some tall cupboards had to be removed from the prison compound in order to make room for additional prisoners, a team of British other ranks under the supervision of a German guard loaded the cupboards on a hand-wagon and transported them to a storage hut in the German quarters. With the agreement of the British soldiers, an officer prisoner was concealed in each of a number of cupboards which were transported to the storage hut outside the prison compound. From there they succeeded in making their escape and, according to my informant, at least two of them were not recaptured by the Germans.

Among the cultural activities of the camp drama and music absorbed the time and interest of a large number of prisoners and gave much pleasure to many others. The success of those interested in dramatic productions was particularly notable, since they began with a bare room in which they built a stage largely from crates which had contained Red Cross parcels; produced furniture and props mainly from the same material; made curtains from bed-sheets; designed and made costumes for male and female characters; designed and installed footlights, spotlights and even dimmers and then staged a series of productions of a remarkably high standard, ranging from classical drama to variety shows and farce, some of which was written in the prison camp.

The theatre was a focus of interest and activity for some of the ablest men in the camp, including a youthful producer and writer of sketches who, in later life, was a minister in Mrs. Thatcher's cabinet and another young man from a prominent family who later was appointed by the Government to chair public bodies and ultimately awarded a life peerage. Productions included *A Midsummer Night's Dream, Arms and the Man, You Never Can Tell, Hay Fever, Present Laughter, Private Lives, Gaslight, Grouse in June, Home and Beauty, Small Bachelor, Love from a Stranger, You Can't Take It With You*, and *The Mikado*, in addition to a Christmas pantomime and variety shows written by members of the theatre group. Despite all the difficulties of dressing, production and staging, most of the productions were of a remarkably high standard and female characters were well played by men. I recall in the presentation of *The Mikado*, the tenor of Nanki Poo was on a slightly higher register than the voice of Yum Yum.

The theatrical group was supported by a number of talented artists, architects, engineers and craftsmen who helped to design and build the stage and props, decorate the theatre, draw and paint scenery, design and make costumes and improvise with limited materials and tools. In addition to their work for the theatre they decorated the dining room and recreation hut and displayed astonishing ingenuity in making gadgets, equipment, maps, tools and materials to aid attempted escapes planned or approved by the cloak and dagger department. They also played a major role in the planning and promotion of a summer fair which occupied almost all the open space in the compound, and in which almost every prisoner in the camp took part.

In music the camp had an orchestra of between thirty and forty musicians, which organised concerts and also supported the theatre group in musical productions. In addition there were several smaller combinations for light music and dance music. The conductor of the main orchestra was a B. Mus. of a university in South Africa and a very talented musician. Concerts of recorded classical music were played weekly in the camp dining hall. As the repertoire was limited by the number of records which prisoners had been able to acquire, the same classical pieces were frequently repeated. Although I am musically quite uneducated, and have limited appreciation of classical music, I listened to a number of pieces with increasing pleasure and feel my pulse quicken when these same pieces, which I regard as old friends, are played at a concert by a modern orchestra.

The open space between the rows of huts in the compound provided sufficient room for team games on which many of the prisoners were specially keen and which were played to a very high standard. Among the prisoners were Springboks from South Africa, All Blacks from New Zealand, and international footballers from Australia and Britain; Davis Cup tennis players; an international fencing champion; an army boxing champion and others who had played sports at a high level. The general standard of sport was impressive compared with the standard which one would expect from a normal group of comparable age and size. The variety of activities and the quality of life in the camp were enriched by the presence and work of doctors, dentists, padres, architects, engineers, university lecturers, teachers, librarians, bookbinders, hairdressers, carpenters, cobblers and tailors, all recruited and almost all volunteers from the body of prisoners.

Almost all my spare time was taken up with the organisation

and administration of educational activities and with the camp library. One of the pleasing features of the camp was the speed with which the library was built up by an accelerating delivery of books. In addition to the books sent to prisoners by their families and friends, the International Red Cross performed an invaluable service by supplying crates of books from Britain, the Commonwealth countries and especially from the U. S. A. In a period of not much more than a year we accumulated a library of up to ten thousand books, many of them specialist books and text books from the U. S. A. which had been so recently published that they were not yet readily available in Britain. We reached a stage where the available shelving was so crowded that a book had to be removed for every new book put on display. From this wealth of books I selected some hundreds to form a text book library which was specially relevant for our more academic courses of education. I became recognised as text book librarian and accepted responsibility for the delivery of text books to prisoners who were following an approved course of study and for retrieving the books from them after a stated interval. This I found to be the only reliable method to ensure circulation of these scarce and much-sought-after books

My principal duty within the camp organisation was to serve as one of two education officers appointed by the Senior British Officer. The senior education officer was an experienced teacher from England who nominated me to serve as junior education officer. Our task was to organise and administer the formal and informal educational activities in the camp. In the organisation of courses leading to recognised academic and professional qualifications our task was complicated by the presence in the camp of officers from Australia, New Zealand, Canada and South Africa as well as from Britain. That we succeeded in arranging suitable courses and recognised examinations for these different national groups was due in large measure to three factors: the variety of course specifications and relevant examination papers despatched to us by the efficient staff of the Bodleian Library in Oxford, which appeared to be the recognised centre in England for the provision of such courses and examination papers to POW camps; the efficiency of the International Red Cross personnel who organised the transmission of educational material through Switzerland and the surprising efficiency of the German postal and rail services in time of war, despite the destruction caused by Allied bombers. I regret that the name of the lady in the Bodleian Library with whom we corresponded has escaped my memory, for I developed great admiration and respect for her unfailing efficiency. Through the services of the Bodleian Library we were able to provide relevant academic courses for the various nationalities in almost any subject which did not require the use of an equipped laboratory, and to set examinations at various levels up to university degree standard. In little over a year we set and invigilated seventy six examinations, and wrote a brief report to accompany the examination papers of each student, stating his nationality, his course of study and the educational status which fitted him to take the examination. About three hundred students followed various academic courses with some degree of success, and from the examinations which we conducted only one examination paper was mislaid. Behind the temporary loss of that single examination paper lies an interesting story which only the senior education officer could relate.

In the conduct of academic courses of study we enjoyed two marked advantages: the first was the relative maturity of our students and their freedom from outside distractions; the second was the number and high quality of the lecturers who were prepared to offer their services as tutors for the benefit of the students. Among the South African officers, most of whom had been taken prisoner when Tobruk was captured by Rommel's forces, were some of the ablest and most highly qualified professional and business men in South Africa. These men, irrespective of age and seniority, had volunteered for military service because they felt an obligation to give active support to the Allied cause, and many of them found satisfaction in making their learning and wisdom available to students.

While the provision of formal courses of study was our main preoccupation, we also took an interest in organising educational activities which might appeal to a wider audience. Because of my interest in Psychology which I had studied for three years prior to 1940, I prepared and delivered a series of informal lectures on the psychology of everyday life, which attracted a fairly good audience. Other informal lecture courses were offered on subjects such as 'Science for the Layman', 'Education for Parents', 'Aspects of Recent History', 'Modern States and Political Theories' and 'Public Speaking'. A number of the most highly qualified officers in the camp were also persuaded to deliver a popular lecture on a subject of their choice, and these attracted an audience large enough to justify holding them in the camp dining hall. Most of these popular lectures were of high quality and their flavour can perhaps best be appreciated by quoting, from notes which I made at the time, the substance of a humorous talk by a South African officer of Scottish extraction.

The Kriegy

A Study in Morbid Psychology.

The Kriegy goes under different names-K. G.; POW; PdeG; or just 'Poor Sucker'. He is conceived in error and born in confusion, for he claims to be the outcome of a mistake committed by a superior being. His life cycle can be divided into three psychological phases: first a period of initiation lasting for some months, and characterised by hunger, dirt and impatience; secondly an indeterminate period of X years whose significant features are food, argument and, perhaps, talk about sex; thirdly the closing stage-shall we say the final twelve months-of which I can say little, for as yet I have had no practical experience.

The Kriegy is born into this life of sin in one of several ways: dug out of the ground; squeezed out of a tin; spewed up like Jonah on some unfriendly beach; or dropped from the sky by the stork in an inverted napkin. He may hatch out at any time, but the two chief spawning seasons seem to be mid-summer and mid-winter, so we may expect another hatching quite soon. The winter species have short, scrubby bristles on the face and a collar of mangy fur around the ears and on the nape of the neck. The grub or embryo Kriegy suffers from acute hydrophobia and, in extreme cases, goes as far as to house large colonies of parasites on his body. On retiring to rest, or hibernate-and here again I refer to the winter variety-he retains all clothing and may make the further addition of a greatcoat, balaclava helmet, muffler, extra socks and newspapers. A fastidious kriegy may unlace his boots or, in extreme cases, remove them.

The chief preoccupation of the kriegy is food-any kind of food. The extraverts may root around like Nebuchadnezzar for edible herbs, explore rubbish heaps, bargain with emissaries of the foreign power for unconsidered trifles, and stalk more opulent or more improvident members of their own species for excreta in the shape of discarded cigarette stumps. The visionaries throw themselves into a trance or state of wild-eyed rapture in which they can envisage gastronomical orgies in some mystical life to come. Such experiences of past or future bliss they communicate with enthusiasm and salivation to less imaginative comrades. An observer may see them perambulating in couples: grave, bearded men in earnest conversation. There go Moses and General Booth; here are Trotski and Karl Marx or is it Socrates and G. B. Shaw planning a new heaven upon earth? Well, not exactly-they are discussing the relative merits of underdone steak and mushrooms or bacon and eggs with buttered toast.

Apart from food their favourite preoccupation is sitting in the sunshine and thinking, or perhaps just sitting, watching for the first signs of a relieving host, the clanking chariots marching over the skyline or the white sails dropping from the clouds. The keynote is impatience; nothing is worth doing for salvation is ever at hand. On the most conservative estimate-no one is more conservative than the Kriegy-he will have departed this life next week or, at most, next month.

I now pass to the second phase: those years of relative stability, acceptance and resignation which are the staple of the Kriegy's life. Physical needs have by now been largely satisfied- all except one which may more properly be classed as a luxury. Whereas the energies of other species of mankind are devoured in a struggle for food, clothing, shelter and possession of a mate or series of mates, it is otherwise with the Kriegy. The Detaining Power presents him with a sufficiency of macaroni, beet tops and frosted tubers, whilst charitable organisations in his own land provide the rest. He is, therefore, a powerful machine, geared to no load and threshing itself to pieces; a ship's turbine with propeller racing free or, if you will, a motor car with a burnt and slipping clutch. This superfluous energy finds several outlets. Most obvious is his favourite pastime-conversation and argument. The Kriegy's most urgent social need is an audience: anything from the confessional to the mass meeting to which he can explain how he was born, how he became a Kriegy. If in his previous existence he was an infantry-man he requires the following: -two or more sardine tins to represent enemy tanks, and to represent himself-a mug, one empty, symbolic mug! If previously an airman, the palms of his hands with fingers free or interlocked are enough. In either case it is a quiet tale of simple heroism, like an old Norse saga. At least it is like a Norse saga in two respects: it is lengthy,. requiring two hours or more if a good gate can be obtained; and it is frequently repeated, certainly around every festive board. It follows a simple formula-a story of quick and accurate thinking; wise advice freely tendered and foolishly rejected by the higher command; loyal obedience to an obdurate superior; frequent use of the phrase: 'There was I——'; and the curtain rung down on tragedy, inevitable and sublime. It is a moving tale-it never fails to move the audience, usually in a hurry!

Noteworthy too is the Kriegy's love of argument, his constant indulgence in disputation. The subjects of argument are innumerable and inexhaustible. I have seen two of the keenest intellects in this camp wager sufficient money to support for one month an unemployed family; I have seen them expose themselves to the gravest danger by climbing over the tripwire into forbidden territory in the face of German machine-guns; and for what purpose: to settle some momentous affair of state? No, simply to establish the nature of the primary characteristics of a prowling white cat. The language in which the Kriegy conducts his disputation is of some importance. Among most species of mankind the guiding precept seems to be: 'Serviter in modo, fortiter in re' or 'The iron hand in the velvet glove' or, even more freely, 'Wrap up your limburger in scented paper'. The kriegy reverses the accepted mode: his words are full of sound and fury, but he is pained and revolted if any significance should be attached to them. 'To slap out' or 'knock out' of people various noxious substances merely implies that one group has established a slight ascendancy over another. Your Kriegy is not content to make a fool out of someone: 'fool' is not strong enough; or consider the Rabelaisian epithet to describe a trivial miscarriage of some prearranged plan. I shrink from pronouncing the term but its homophone is 'a real muck-up!'

Time does not permit to deal with the kriegy's other habits: how he drives his galleries and despoils the fixtures and fittings until his home is like an overripe cheese and his bed a mere toe hold; or his liking for rumours, grapevines, latrinograms; or his queues, the something for nothing impulse or the desire to be first in line: he will even queue up to be first into a cattle truck! I should have liked to have said something about his games, and also about his music, crooned out in noisome latrines. Much could be said about his accounts of his social background and his former incarnations in which he invariably held an important and lucrative position. His children, if he admits to any, are witty, wise and gifted, all top of the class; a serious problem if the ranks become more swollen. Again there is his unfailing optimism which tells him at any period of his present predicament that within three months he is sure to be translated to a better world. One last point: the Kriegy labours under a fundamental, calamitous disability-a disability that he shares with the banana, the mule and the male soprano-the Kriegy as a Kriegy cannot reproduce his own species. Whether he may be able to do so in that hypothetical future life for which he so eagerly longs is a riddle whose solution is mercifully hidden from our eyes".

The talk by my friend from South Africa paints an amusing caricature of the kriegsgefangener or prisoner of war, but like all good caricatures it is a revealing picture of the characteristic features of the subject. From personal experience and from watching other prisoners I can confirm that a period of deep depression, and perhaps even shame, was a normal reaction to being taken prisoner or 'put in the bag'. While everyone engaged in active service on any battle front had perforce to accept the possibility of death or serious disability, the normal attitude to the possibility of being taken prisoner was to believe that this might happen to other people but would certainly not happen to you. When it did happen the conditions were such as to make capture inevitable, short of committing suicide, (and in my case ensuring the death of my crew) but that did not make it any the more bearable or any the less humiliating. The initial reaction for most people, especially officers in charge of men, was a period of depression and introspection when both the present and the future appeared to be black beyond description. Depending on the personality, temperament and inner resources of the individual, the initial period of wallowing in gloom and depression varied in duration and in modes of expression. Some fell into such depths of inactivity that personal hygiene was neglected and even getting out of bed demanded more energy than they could muster. Others after a period of silence developed a compulsion to justify themselves and to absolve themselves of all responsibility for their capture. Fortunately for most prisoners the initial period of depression was brief and soon gave way to a healthy endeavour to make the best of a bad situation, to cultivate friendships and to engage in such physical and social activities as their restricted conditions would permit.

From the date of my capture by Rommel's troops until my group of prisoners settled down in Oflag 5a at Weinsberg in Germany, our existence was such as to give little opportunity for the development of cultural and social activities. In the POW cage at Tunis and at the transit camp in Capua books, paper, games equipment and social amenities were totally lacking; many of the prisoners were depressed and still trying to recover from the shock of being captured; social cohesion was still minimal; food was so deficient in quantity and quality as to discourage physical effort and stomach troubles were rife. When we were transferred to the permanent camp at Modena we found ourselves confined in separate barrack rooms with little opportunity except at mealtimes to meet and socialise with the occupants of other barrack rooms. Books and games equipment were minimal, for we received no supply of books through the International Red Cross, and when books were sent to prisoners by relatives the Italian authorities almost destroyed them by ripping off the covers and spine to search for concealed messages or other hidden material. The food supplied and cooked by the Italians was so inadequate that the prisoners had to rely on Red Cross parcels to supply much of their essential nourishment, and in Italy the supply of parcels was irregular and unpredictable. Much of our time was spent trying to cook food from our parcels on tiny improvised cooking stoves made largely from food tins and fuelled with scraps of wood, some of which came from the slats on our beds.

When the delivery of food parcels was delayed and irregular, due perhaps to the incompetence of the Italian authorities, or perhaps to the effects of bombing by allied aircraft, hunger was so pervasive in the camp that thoughts of food and longing for food became an obsession. While the contents of food parcels varied, each box usually contained a packet of twenty cigarettes and a quarter-pound bar of chocolate. Swapping of food items was a regular practice to satisfy variable preferences, and as I was a nonsmoker I initially swapped cigarettes for a bar of chocolate.

Long before the end of my period of captivity I began to swap my block of chocolate for a packet of cigarettes because, in periods of hunger, I tended to eat the chocolate within hours of receiving the parcel, whereas I found that smoking a cigarette with a cup of ersatz tea or coffee, brewed from seeds collected from herbs and bushes, was a reasonably effective remedy to quell for a time the pangs of hunger. At the age of over thirty I became a cigarette smoker and continued until my retirement when I was able to defeat the habit. Incidentally I can recall that Red Cross parcels packed in Scotland usually contained a tin of oatmeal for which I willingly swapped almost any other item, except Canadian powdered milk called 'Klim', for I liked oatmeal porridge and I found by experience that a tin of oatmeal would make several satisfying helpings of porridge, for which Klim supplied the milk.

When our group of prisoners finally settled in Oflag 5a at Weinsberg in Germany, I was allocated to a room occupied by fourteen men of whom the majority were English, leavened by a few Scots and Welshmen. Occasionally the number grew to sixteen when the camp was overcrowded, and we had to live together in these cramped surroundings for a period of about eighteen months. The total population of the prison compound, which comprised an area of about four hundred by one hundred metres, varied between 1100 and 1200 people, including the other ranks. Every day in the morning, at midday and at sundown the German guards, with at least one officer in command, conducted a meticulous roll-call, when the prisoners were lined up in hut groups in the open courtyard of the compound and were counted by the guards. After the evening roll-call the prisoners were locked in their huts until morning roll-call, and in winter that extended up to fifteen hours of incarceration. If one or more prisoners had attempted an escape or if a tunnel were discovered by the Germans, a special roll-call was held when the prisoners could be kept standing in the open air, irrespective of weather conditions, for hours on end. During such periods the German officers and guards were subjected to almost continuous abuse and sarcastic comment from the lines of prisoners, who were increasingly confident as the months passed that the German military forces were doomed to inevitable defeat.

Despite the trying conditions in which we had to live I found that a POW camp provided a good environment in which to study the reactions and behaviour of men who were compelled to live for a long period within a rigid framework of rules imposed by the German authorities and in cramped, confined and overcrowded conditions. If a large body of young, active, vigorous and intelligent men are shut up for a long period in cramped, uncomfortable quarters will they live peaceably with one another or will they finally get at each other's throats? If they have no opportunity to engage in their normal work, how will they occupy themselves? Will they make work for themselves, spend most of their time in amusement and sport, sink into laziness and lethargy or turn in on themselves and suffer from melancholia and depression? When a group of mainly young, healthy, vigorous men are segregated for a long period from all female society do they brood, become intensely irritable, display some of the signs of thwarted lovers or develop homosexual relationships? When a large group of men are thrust into an empty camp, with no cultural or social amenities and minimal help from outwith the camp, how do they organise themselves, in what kind of activities do they engage and what kind of cultural and social life do they develop?

I found it interesting to compare the reactions of our group to the discomforts, limitations and privations of prison life with the descriptions which I have read of men who had to live together over long periods, cut off from their fellows and subject to conditions that imposed on them more than usual hardships. There are many examples in literature as well as in real life. Under extreme conditions there is always a danger that the veneer of civilisation and culture will be ripped off and that the baser instincts of cruelty and selfishness will emerge. There is a risk in forcing a group of men to endure too much of each other's company in conditions of prolonged deprivation, hardship and boredom. Imagine a group of fourteen to sixteen active, young men locked up night after night in one room with minimal heating, poor lighting, stools with no back-rests as the only seats, sharing lockers, sleeping in two-tiered bunks from which many of the supporting slats had been removed to line tunnels or for other purposes, crowded round one central table, perhaps short of food and tobacco due to the non-arrival of Red Cross parcels, and missing news from home because the mail had been delayed or destroyed by bombing. One would expect such a situation to breed bad feeling, disagreement, irritation, smouldering dislikes and periodic explosions of temper, which occasionally did occur. The periodic explosion was sometimes the safest reaction, because it relieved suppressed feelings and helped to clear the air.

Having lived in such a situation for a lengthy period I can confirm that the risk of explosion produced interesting defence mechanisms which ensured a remarkable degree of harmony and tolerance. One of the most effective defence mechanisms was for everyone to develop a lively interest in some cultural, practical or social activity. If hands and minds were kept occupied, feelings were usually under much better control and tempers were more relaxed. Another effective defence mechanism was to foster at all times the spirit, if not the meticulous forms, of courtesy and consideration for others. Living in these conditions, when petty selfishness could readily have prevailed, it was pleasing to find how generous men could be, and such acts of generosity were even more valuable in conditions of severe deprivation than in ordinary social life. In our room no one ever received a parcel from home without offering to share anything which could be shared. Such generosity was almost deliberately cultivated in the knowledge that it preserved the social decencies and enhanced the family atmosphere.

We have all heard or read of people living far from the comforts of civilisation who made a habit of bathing and shaving every day and, in some cases, dressing for dinner. Such stories illustrate a vital truth. If one is constrained to live in conditions which fall far below accustomed standards, when washing and shaving can be done only in acute discomfort; where there seems no incentive to dress decently; where drabness and squalor are the normal conditions of living, it is all too easy to fall away from normal civilised habits and it is specially important, when living in a community to maintain personal discipline and preserve the routine of cleanliness and neatness, decency in dress and general deportment and consideration for others in the group. Fortunately my companions did maintain good standards of personal care and room hygiene and, in general, the longer they were held prisoner the higher did their personal standards and their consideration for others become.

It was not uncommon for prisoners who had recently been captured to allow their standards of personal hygiene, dress and deportment to slip, but that was a normal reaction to the shock of being taken prisoner from which most people recovered within a relatively short period. Sometimes lack of normal hygiene was a mere foible. I recall an occasion when I developed serious digestive trouble from particularly coarse food supplied by the German authorities and had to visit the camp medical centre. While I was detained there coffee brewed from the usual herbal mixture was served and I had omitted to bring my tin mug. A senior officer from South Africa who, in civilian life, was a prominent architect, kindly offered to lend me a mug which was filled with coffee. When I had drunk some of the liquid the mug appeared to be so filthy that I took it to a washbasin, discarded the remains of the coffee, and found that the mug was so coated and discoloured as to defy cleaning. I took it to a fire-bucket of coarse sand which was stored in the corridor, scrubbed it thoroughly with sand and then washed it. When I returned it to the major with thanks, he was engaged in playing poker, glanced at the mug and said it was not his. When I explained how I had scoured and cleaned it, he became quite annoyed and exclaimed; 'Good God, you have ruined it. That mug has not been washed since I arrived here, for a good coating is essential to put some flavour into that bloody ersatz coffee!'

Before becoming a prisoner I thought I knew what hunger was, but in fact most of us who live in a comfortable home have known only the pleasant side of hunger. Hunger is but the prelude to a good and satisfying meal. A POW camp was a good place in which to observe the effects of hunger on a group of men, although a prison camp in Europe certainly could not compare with a prison camp in the far East. In my experience the first prolonged bout of hunger that one suffers is by far the worst, especially if one has previously been well fed. Some people, after long practice, can school themselves to master and ignore constant pain; but to the majority it is as difficult to ignore prolonged hunger as it is to ignore severe toothache or headache. When hunger is really prolonged it can become an obsession which prevents one from thinking of any other subject for any length of time. All one's attention and energy become absorbed in the craving for food, just as probably happens with the hungry animal which goes on the hunt for prey.

At later stages in our prison life long periods of hunger coincided with periods when Red Cross parcels failed to arrive, probably due to destruction of the railway system by Allied air attacks. When parcels were in good supply each prisoner received one parcel per week, and that probably provided at least half of the food value of the weekly diet. When for any reason the supply of food parcels was seriously interrupted, the camp was stricken with deep depression. By that time, however, our stomachs had become accustomed to less nourishment; perhaps the flow of digestive juices had decreased and the pangs of hunger were more easily borne; but when food became really scarce it was the one absorbing topic of thought and conversation.

When food parcels were being delivered at regular weekly intervals, most of us learned by bitter experience to save some food against the inevitable lean times. In order to prevent prisoners from hoarding tins of food as an aid towards escape plans, the German guards were ordered to ensure that all food tins were pierced before the parcels were delivered to the prison huts, but occasionally an unpierced tin was delivered and was usually carefully hoarded by the prisoner who received it. In a period of scarcity most prisoners used their small hoard of food with care and discretion, although it could occasionally lead to trouble. One of the ludicrous incidents of which I heard related to a young officer from Australia, who had been in hospital on a very meagre diet. He emerged convalescent at a time of food scarcity and turned to his small hoard which apparently consisted of a tin of butter, two packets of raisins and a tin of condensed milk which had not been pierced. He opened the tins and packets, creamed the whole mixture in a mess tin and ate as much as he could. Within a few hours he was back in hospital and it was said that only the prompt use of a stomach pump saved his life. He was kept in hospital for some time on a diet of nothing but liquids.

Just as we in our normal well-fed condition find it difficult fully to appreciate the physical and psychological effects of prolonged hunger, so I am inclined to think that in our normal mixed society we may find it difficult to assess the physical and psychological effects of prolonged segregation from all feminine company on a group of active, healthy, vigorous young men. I have been too well nourished on the doctrines of Freud and other psychoanalysts to belittle the crucial importance of sexual activity in human life, where biologically, psychologically and socially it obviously plays a major role. In our prison camp, however, I formed the impression that the effects of segregating a body of energetic, healthy, intelligent young men and compelling them for a long period to lead a monastic life were not nearly as dramatic or disruptive of their emotional and social life as one might suppose. From my own experience and from what I could gather from observation and discussion with others, the experience imposed on the majority surprisingly little conscious psychological tension. The conclusion which I formed (and it was not solely my own finding) was that so long as women are completely removed from their orbit and there is no opportunity to mix with them, men can manage to live without them surprisingly well. I note that this conclusion was confirmed by Alan Moorhead in his book on Montgomery. Describing the Eighth Army in the desert he noted their apparent self-sufficiency and freedom from the trammels of sex.

Certainly in our monastic life there was a tendency to form an intimate friendship with a special buddy with whom men shared most of their thoughts, and with whom they argued and sometimes quarrelled and made it up. The tendency to have a buddy was more marked in the armed forces than in civilian life, and was perhaps more marked in POW camp than in the forces. In certain cases and with certain types the tendency to have a special pal developed into what was known as a 'beautiful friendship'. Sometimes a 'beautiful friendship' was between an obviously male and a rather female type; but more often both parties were rather sensitive, feminine types and their close friendship was probably a means of mutual protection in a fairly 'butch' environment. Only rarely did such friendships become embarrassing, although on my rounds as textbook librarian, I once observed a young man sitting by the bunk of another who was reclining at ease and stroking his hair as they talked.

What was the general psychological effect of POW life? Were prisoners more liable to mental and emotional instability than men on active service or in civilian life? To these questions I am in no position to give categorical answers. The majority of people appeared to stand up remarkably well to the strains and stresses of POW existence, just as most people did to the demands of the front line on land, sea and air. Some found the strain heavy and were perhaps permanently marked by it; a few cracked up. One thing which struck me was that, apart from the obviously unstable or neurotic type of person, it was almost impossible to spot beforehand the man who was liable to break down and, conversely, the one who positively thrived when the action got hot or when conditions imposed the greatest stress. That was specially true in battle but was also true of men in POW camps. Under the peculiar conditions of prison camp I found that there were two types of people who found life especially difficult and who were liable to age and become shrunken before one's eyes. One was the type of person who, for some reason, failed to find in prison camp any activity which held and absorbed his interest. In sheer self -defence one had to cultivate interests and hobbies and ways of passing the time, because most of us had too much time on our hands. The majority succeeded; a few failed and the result for those few could be permanent boredom and depression, which made them fall in on themselves and shrink both physically and spiritually.

The other and more surprising type were those who, for some reason, gained the impression that they were forgotten men and brooded on that conviction. In most instances the impression was quite mistaken and a pure delusion. Perhaps letters from home were not coming through regularly, or parcels from home failed to reach them, or they formed the rooted conviction that their wife or girl friend had gone off the rails; but at any rate they suffered from the belief that they were forgotten, unwanted and nobody loved them. In the camp one heard occasional whispers that someone had received a 'Dear John' letter. If in any instance such gossip were based on fact, it could explain the kind of hopeless depression which I have tried to describe.

Towards the end of the war news began filtering through to us that families at home were being given helpful advice on how to treat the returned POW. The gist of the stories which reached us was that relatives and friends should expect us to be rather queer, probably not very sociable, inclined to wish to be alone, to shrink from meeting people outwith the immediate family and inclined to be moody and irritable. Such stories became a stock source of jokes around the camp. One of our favourite themes was taunting each other with just how far 'round the bend' we were. The extreme case was to tell a friend that he was so far round the bend that he was beginning to see his own rear light! Rather to our surprise some of us found when we arrived home that we did tend to display for a time some of the symptoms that our families had apparently been advised to expect.

Chapter 14
From War to Peace

IN 1944 A PARTY OF prisoners on their return from a convalescent period at an outside camp succeeded by a clever ruse in smuggling past the German guards a radio which enabled us to receive regular news broadcasts from Britain. The morale of the prisoners in the camp was progressively raised as it became increasingly obvious by the news from both the Eastern and Western fronts that the German forces were facing ultimate defeat. To us the clearest evidence of Allied dominance was the bombardment by day and night of German cities and industrial centres by fleets of American and British bombers. By the beginning of 1945 the numbers of American bombers, supported by fighter planes, were sometimes such as to blot out the sunlight and create a cloudy sky with their vapour trails, as they flew high over the camp on a bombing mission. At night we repeatedly heard bomber squadrons flying overhead, and the flash and roar of explosives were cheered when the objectives of the bombers were within sight and sound of the camp. By the early Spring of 1945 the environs of the camp were occasionally strafed by fast fighter planes when stray rounds did not always miss the prison compound. For that reason our other ranks were assigned the task of digging slit trenches in which the prisoners could take shelter when air-raid warnings were sounded. I recall that on more than one occasion the senior education officer and I had to interrupt an examination which we were invigilating to enable the examinees to take shelter in the slit trenches. The times when the examinations were stopped and started were carefully noted in order to maintain the correct period of examination.

In April, 1945, the German Camp Commandant informed the Senior British Officer that all the prisoners, the German staff and families were to be transferred by train to a new location. The planned move raised considerable misgivings among the prisoners, because rumours had begun to circulate that, as a last desperate gamble, Hitler had planned a final stand in the mountainous terrain of Austria and Bavaria and that officer prisoners, in particular, were to be transferred to these locations and held as hostages. Because of the obvious weakness of the German position the Senior British Officer insisted that a large red cross be painted on the roof of every railway carriage to be used for the transfer of prisoners under his charge. As this precaution would also improve the prospects of protecting the German personnel from Allied air attack the proposition was accepted by the German Commandant.

As space aboard the train was strictly limited much of our personal belongings and most of the material, including library books and theatrical equipment which we had accumulated, had perforce to be abandoned in the camp. I recall packing a large cardboard box with assorted belongings, including lecture notes and summaries of textbooks which I had read, binding it with wire and scrawling my wife's address in several places. Much to my amazement the whole package, completely intact, was delivered to Kilcreggan on the Firth of Clyde some months later. In tribute to the military forces perhaps I should record that a canvas bag and contents, which I discarded from my tank before moving into the battle in Tunisia in which I was taken prisoner, was also safely returned to my wife's home in Kilcreggan and I still retain it as a memento.

After a much-interrupted train journey, which lasted for the better part of two days, we were all much relieved when, instead of penetrating the mountainous country of Austria, the train drew into a station to the North of Munich and we were herded into a camp at Moosburg, which must by that time have been one of the largest POW camps in Germany, with a population perhaps exceeding 50,000 prisoners. The main reason for the slow and intermittent journey by rail had been the frequency of air-raid alerts when the train halted for long periods in the shelter of tunnels, and also the severity of the damage caused by air raids which had left railway stations and sidings devastated, with wrecked carriages piled on top of wrecked carriages and, in some instances, wrecked engines piled on top of wrecked engines. Merely to keep the rail track open must have demanded herculean efforts by German and conscripted workmen. That the population of Germany had been prepared or compelled to endure so much for so many years appeared to me to bear ample testimony to the iron grip of the military and police machine built up by the Nazis.

By the Spring of 1945 the huge camp at Moosburg must have held prisoners from almost every nation which had fought, or been occupied by, the armed forces of Germany. From the Soviet Union through Eastern Europe to the Atlantic, the United States and the countries of the Commonwealth which had supported Britain representatives of their peoples, in varying numbers, could be found immured in one or more of the numerous prison cages at Moosburg. The most interesting whom I found were officers of the Fifty-First Highland Division who had been taken prisoner at St Valery in May, 1940, and had spent five weary years as prisoners of war. To me it came as a shock of pleasant surprise to find how well they had maintained their morale and physical fitness and how neatly they were dressed, many wearing kilts and jackets which may have been sent to them by their families. On one evening in the camp a group of these officers, with bagpipe accompaniment, gave a display of Highland dancing which seemed to me to match the standards of competitive dancing which I had often witnessed at Highland Games in Argyllshire, and which was clear evidence of their meticulous training in technique and of their athletic fitness.

A much less agreeable aspect of our brief sojourn at Moosburg was the atmosphere of hostility which prevailed, not only between the prisoners and their German guards, but also among the groups of prisoners from the various nationalities of Eastern Europe. Most of the prisoners from Britain, the Commonwealth countries and the United States had a somewhat tolerant attitude towards the people of all nationalities and, even towards the Germans, the hostility was a product of war rather than an ingrained state of implacable enmity and hatred. The impression gained from admittedly limited mixing with the prisoners of other nationalities was radically different. The hostility between the Russian prisoners and their German guards was to be expected and, by that final stage of the war, the Germans obviously feared the Russians more than they feared any other nationality. The prisoners from what was then known as the Balkans not only hated the Germans and distrusted the Russians, but most of them also disliked and distrusted each other. The Polish prisoners gave the impression that they hated and distrusted every other nationality. When I discussed these ingrained attitudes of hostility with a few obviously well-educated and intelligent prisoners who were reasonably fluent in English, I heard various explanations, two of which seemed to me to be particularly compelling. The first was that the prolonged invasion and occupation of a country or territory by the armed forces of another country inevitably resulted in growing hostility to the occupying power and its people. In general the more prolonged the occupation the more implacable grew the hostility. The second compelling explanation of hostility was probably related to the first, in that it became obvious to me that for the great majority of men the deepest hatred and loathing are engendered by the rape and maltreatment, or even the seduction, of their women and children. The argument was put to me that the British found it difficult to understand, much less share, the depth of hostility and even gut hatred felt by the peoples of Eastern Europe for people of other nationalities because for many centuries the British did not have to suffer the indignity and humiliation of being occupied by the armed forces of a foreign power.

In the first week of May, 1945, the POW camp at Moosburg was relieved by American troops under the command of General Patton. As the numbers and various nationalities of the prisoners were such as to make it impracticable for the relatively small force of American troops to exert military discipline in the camp, the hostility to which I have referred was amply demonstrated when groups of prisoners swarmed over the surrounding countryside and slaughtered every creature they could find, including farm animals. The families who occupied the houses in the local village, many of whom may have been the families of camp guards and others employed in the camp, tried to safeguard themselves by inviting officer prisoners to take up temporary residence in their houses. Judging from the information which I was able to gather, the German residents had a strong preference for British officers to be their temporary guests and protectors. I found this information reassuring because it seemed to indicate that, despite the years of hostile propaganda poured out by the Nazi Government, the ordinary people of Germany were still prepared to trust the

British to maintain civilised standards of behaviour. It was all the more galling, therefore, when a British NCO on the plane which I boarded at Moosburg boastfully displayed in his kitbag all the silver sacramental plate from the local church. When some of us expressed displeasure he shrugged it off with the remark that if he had not taken it some other prisoner certainly would have done.

With a demonstration of their remarkable ability to organise transport, the American forces within a few days provided a small fleet of Dakota aircraft to fly the Allied prisoners from a grass strip near Moosburg to a military air base near Brussels. There we were washed, had our clothing sprayed with insecticide powder and those of us who were British were handed over to the RAF. By what means the majority of the British and Commonwealth prisoners were flown to Britain I know not, but I was one of a small group who were packed into the empty body of a Lancaster bomber where we sprawled on the metal floor in darkness during our flight to an air base in England of which the identity was not made known to us. After a short delay we each received a travel pass which enabled us to travel home by rail. In company with a few Scottish prisoners I travelled to Edinburgh where, at a military depot, I was allowed to choose a civilian suit and received an issue of underwear. I was then free to go my own way on what was termed 'release leave.'

For the first time since the prison camp at Moosburg had been relieved by General Patton's troops, I was able to get in touch with my wife to inform her that I had been released from POW camp, that I had arrived in Edinburgh and that I hoped within a few hours to reach Kilcreggan. The train journey from Edinburgh to Glasgow and Gourock and the short ferry crossing from Gourock to Kilcreggan seemed to take a long time, but when I stepped on to the pier at Kilcreggan there was my wife to greet me along with our son Kenneth. That was one of the high points of my life.

Only much later did it occur to me to wonder how Kenneth managed to adjust to my arrival. Here was this bright and sensitive boy, now in his third year, who had from birth been the centre of the attention, care and love of his mother and now, suddenly, had to accept the presence of a stranger, not merely as a permanent addition to the family but as a rival for the affection and care of his mother. Although his mother had no doubt done her best to let him know about his father and that some day he would come home, it must still for a child of his age have taken time to accept the major change in the family. In retrospect it is pleasant to record that, if hurt was caused, it was by no means permanent and that I was soon accepted as father of the family.

It appeared that the families of those men who had been prisoners of war for a considerable period really had been advised that, after their release, some prisoners might display symptoms of psychological disturbance and emotional trauma. If I exhibited such symptoms my wife was sufficiently wise and tolerant to accept them as temporary and draw no attention to them. Rather more troublesome were the physical disabilities which had been mainly if not wholly caused by the privations of life in prison camps. For some years after the war I was subject to periodic outbreaks of boils, which were resistant to treatment but gradually ameliorated and finally ceased. The coarse vegetables and stale rye bread which formed the bulk of our diet in Germany proved to be too difficult for my digestive system to absorb, with the result that I was compelled towards the end of 1944 to seek medical attention from the camp doctors. With the cooperation of the German authorities the doctors were finally able to arrange my attendance for X-ray examination at a hospital in Heilbronn, as a result of which a report was sent to the camp medical centre that I had developed a gastric ulcer. For this condition the doctors in the camp could provide only limited treatment, and I had to live with bouts of more or less severe pain.

When I returned home I was so content to spend a quiet life with my family that I took no steps to report my medical condition. I can only assume that a report reached the War Office either from the medical records of Oflag 5a at Weinsberg or from the hospital at Heilbronn, for much to my surprise I received an instruction to report at a military hospital situated in Buchanan Castle, Drymen. There I spent the better part of two weeks undergoing thorough medical examination, following which a report was sent to the War Department confirming that I had developed a gastric ulcer. After due consideration of this report and of the duration of my period as a POW, the War Department decided to award me a partial disability pension amounting to one-third of a full pension. Some two years later, when I was appointed to a post as director of education, the pension was promptly terminated, although the ulcer continued to trouble me for almost ten years when it suddenly cured itself and has not recurred during the past forty years.

In the second week of August I received a letter from the War Office instructing me to report to an address in London for interview. It transpired that the interview by a senior officer was to assess my fitness for military service in the Far East, where the war against Japan had not yet reached its climax. On the train journey South from Glasgow I read with a shock of surprise in the morning newspaper the first report of the dropping of an atomic bomb on the Japanese city of Hiroshima. The possibility, much less the existence, of an atomic bomb was something of which I had been entirely ignorant. When I arrived at my destination in London I was received by a Colonel who expressed sympathy about my ulcer, but then spent rather more time deploring his transfer from active service in the field, coincidentally because he also had developed an ulcer. Towards the end of a pleasant interview the Colonel asked me if I wished to resume my civilian occupation as soon as opportunity offered. When I replied in the affirmative he smiled and, after a brief discussion of the probable effects of the dropping of an atomic bomb on a Japanese city, he imitated my Scottish accent and said: 'I would advise you to return home, laddie; I should be surprised if you were called upon to serve in the Far East.'

Reassured by my interview in London and wishing to test the market on prospects of securing employment other than class teaching in Glasgow, I immediately began to submit applications for posts in the field of Education. Probably because of my early release from prison camp, and because men of my age and academic qualifications were still liable to be engaged in military service, I found myself on three short lists all at the same time: two for posts of assistant director of education and one as a lecturer in Educational Psychology. The first interview was that for assistant director of education in the County of Fife to which I was fortunate enough to be appointed. That appointment as the junior member of an excellent administrative team settled my future career. After an apprenticeship of rather less than two years in Fife I spent the next twenty eight years as a director of education: eight years in Berwickshire, followed by twenty years in the Combined County of Perth and Kinross, from which I retired when Local Government was reorganised on a regional basis in 1975. During a period of change and expansion in Education, including the raising of the school leaving age to fifteen and subsequently to sixteen; a continuous programme of school building; improvements in provision for handicapped children and slow learners; changes in content and methods of teaching in primary and secondary schools; improvements in furnishings, equipment and teaching aids; provision for greater centralisation, changes in organisation and much larger numbers of pupils in secondary schools; major changes in leaving certificate examinations; a massive increase in provision for formal and informal further education, including new buildings, a continuous increase in the number, variety and standard of courses and a continuous increase in the number of full-time and part-time students; improvements in the staffing of schools and in the provision of advisory staff and a continuous endeavour to improve the relationships of education authorities and their administrative staff with the staffs of the schools and colleges of further education, I for my part found it a strenuous but satisfying career.

Index